WHAT MARILYN SAID ABOUT HER MEN:

THE KENNEDY BROTHERS:
"I'm tired of being used. I'm going public with everything."

FRANK SINATRA:
"The most fascinating man I ever dated. When I'm with him, I feel like I don't have to take pills. He makes me feel secure and happy. He's the only man that's taught me how to love life."

CLARK GABLE:
"I was so thrilled when he kissed me. We had to do the scene over several times. Then the sheet dropped and he put his hand on me. I got goosebumps all over. That night I didn't need sleeping pills."

JOE DIMAGGIO:
"He was the best equipped. The greatest. If our marriage was only sex, it would last forever."

HER MANY ONE-NIGHT STANDS:
"I was happy because I made them happy."

St. Martin's Paperbacks titles are available at quantity discounts for sales promotions, premiums or fund raising. Special books or book excerpts can also be created to fit specific needs.

For information write to special sales manager, St. Martin's Press, 175 Fifth Avenue, New York, N.Y. 10010.

Marilyn's MEN

THE PRIVATE LIFE OF

Marilyn Monroe

JANE ELLEN WAYNE

ST. MARTIN'S PAPERBACKS

First published in Great Britain by Robson Books Ltd.

MARILYN'S MEN

Copyright © 1992 by Jane Ellen Wayne.

Cover photographs courtesy of The Bettmann Archive.

Library of Congress Catalog Card Number: 92-3150

ISBN: 0-312-92943-9

Printed in the United States of America

St. Martin's Press hardcover edition/August 1992
St. Martin's Paperbacks edition/February 1993

10 9 8 7 6 5 4 3 2 1

To Bob Slatzer . . .
   who knew Marilyn best during
   her adult life; confidant,
   husband and close friend.

Contents

Acknowledgments

I would like to thank Robert Slatzer for the many hours spent helping me gather information for this book. Not only is Bob a Monroe historian, he was married to her briefly in 1952. However, he takes just as much pride in being Marilyn's close friend for sixteen years and opening the investigation into her mysterious death.

Also, a note of gratitude to Bob's beautiful companion, Deborah Thompson, who helped me when he was busy with his miniseries "Marilyn and Me" and his exhibit of new Monroe photos taken during the unfinished *Something's Got to Give*.

The list of people who have contributed to the myth and mystery of Marilyn Monroe is a long one, but each deserves mention:

James Bacon, Max Block, Jeanne Carmen, Jack Clemmons, Noble "Kid" Chissel, Jack Cole, Joan Crawford, John Danoff, Peter Dye, Brian Evans, Judith Exner, Tay Garnett, Eleanor "Bebe" Goddard, Deborah Gould, Sheila Graham, Fred Lawrence Guiles, Joe Hyams, Roger Kahn, Patricia Seaton Lawford, Natasha Lytess, Norman Mailer, Eunice Murray, John Miner, Chuck O'Brien, Sir Laurence Olivier, Fred Otash, Lena Pepitone, Mickey Rooney, Jane Russell, Hal Schaefer, Sandra Shevey, Sidney Skolsky, Allan "Whitey" Snyder, James Spada, Milo Speriglio, Gloria Steinem, Michael J. Sullivan, Anthony Summers, Peter Summers, Gene Tierney, Billy Travilla, Leigh Wiener, Billy Wilder, Billy Woodfield, Sam Yorty, Maurice Zolotow.

Academy of Motion Picture Arts and Sciences, Los Angeles;

Beverly Hills Library; F.H. Goldwyn Library, Hollywood;
Library of Performing Arts at Lincoln Center, New York; New
York Public Library; Seek Information Service, Glendale,
California; UCLA Cinema Collection Library, Los Angeles;
USC Main Library—Special Cinema Collection, Los Angeles;
the *New York Post*, the *Los Angeles Times*, the *Los Angeles
Herald-Examiner*, the *New York Times*, the *New York Daily News*,
the *New York Journal—American*, the *New York Mirror*, *People*
magazine, *Life* magazine, *Time* magazine, British Broadcasting
Corporation, *Vanity Fair*, American Movie Classics, the Fox
Network, The Kennedy Library.

Thanks to Pat Wilks Battle at the *New York Post* for providing
me with clippings from national and international news files,
and to movie historian Philip Paul for his valuable help with
research.

I want to express my appreciation to Tom McCormack,
Chairman and C.E.O. of St. Martin's Press, Jeremy Robson,
Chairman of Robson Books in England and his editor Louise
Dixon, to my proficient editor Charles Spicer and his assistant
Geoffrey Kloske, and to Tim James for his legal guidance.
Thanks to Albert Togut for giving me the use of his Manhattan
law offices and to my daughter Elizabeth Jo Wayne, who helped
organize my script revision.

I am also indebted to noted authors C. David Heymann, John
H. Davis and John Austin for their generous endorsements of
Marilyn's Men.

As always, I am grateful to my old friends who worked behind
the scenes in Hollywood. Joan Crawford referred to them as the
"little people who are bigger than life." They contribute
without credit or fanfare, and I respect their anonymity.

Jane Ellen Wayne
New York City

Marilyn's MEN

Preface

There is no dearth of books about Marilyn Monroe, but the men in her life have been vaguely portrayed. Who among them molded her image? Used her? Loved her? Rejected her? Understood her?

Who among them suffered from Marilyn's ambition? Her infidelity? Her tortured soul? Her impassiveness? Her dualism? Her myth?

Baseball hero Joe DiMaggio and playwright Arthur Miller were the dullest chapters in Marilyn's life story. Both men were astute, obstinate, self-contained, and not easily conquered by a sensual woman. To understand their psyches is a novel looksee into Monroe's complexity.

What about the men who did not return Marilyn's love? She carried a torch a long time for her vocal coach Fred Karger – some say forever. Actor Yves Montand bowed out before his wife Simone Signoret threatened divorce. Frank Sinatra bought emeralds for Marilyn, but not a wedding band. The Kennedy brothers had more to lose than any of the others, and they dropped her cold turkey. Marilyn's addiction to Bobby ended her life.

Monroe had more than her share of lovers. She rivaled Joan Crawford and Ava Gardner. Crawford stalked, pounced and then dismissed. Gardner was passionate, possessive and soon bored. But Marilyn did not have the cold and calculating mind of a shrew. She never lost her inner warmth or little-girl qualities despite the bosomy, hip-swaying image.

The love of Ava Gardner's life was Frank Sinatra, but they

could not live under the same roof without raising it. During their marriage, she aborted his baby. Monroe and DiMaggio suffered the same fate, but both couples remained soulmates until the end.

Ava and Marilyn claimed they wanted children desperately, but intimates swear this was not true. Maintaining their exotic figures came first and in Marilyn's case, she feared her child might inherit the mental instability in her family genes. It was Johnny Hyde, a powerful Hollywood agent, who told Marilyn early in her career not to have children. Her tubes were tied, but later she had the operation reversed. Marilyn's affair with Johnny was bittersweet. He launched the Monroe legend, but did not live long enough to see his dream fulfilled.

Her sudden elopement with screenwriter Robert Slatzer in October of 1952 was a well-kept secret. Though Marilyn and Bob had dated frequently for six years, marriage was never mentioned. Slatzer admits they were on an all-night binge, but quite sober on October 4 in Tijuana, Mexico. When Fox mogul Darryl F. Zanuck found out, he told the newlyweds that the studio had too much money invested in Monroe's single image. Zanuck demanded they get an annulment. Bob and Marilyn returned to Mexico and the records were destroyed, but not their close friendship. It was Slatzer who opened the investigation into Marilyn's death that intensifies to this day.

No one has done an in-depth biographical sketch of Robert Slatzer, who was (and still is) intensely devoted to Marilyn. Among the secrets that she shared with him was her diary about Bobby Kennedy. If Slatzer had not been out of town on the weekend of Monroe's death, he might have been her lifeline.

Marilyn was dating Joe DiMaggio when she married Slatzer, who did not consider the Yankee Clipper a big threat to him. One evening Marilyn made dates with both men. She invited them in, quarreled bitterly with Joe, and told them both to leave. Her description of DiMaggio was "dull and possessive." While he pursued Marilyn, she played the field with Johnnie Ray, designer Billy Travilla, Eddie Robinson, Jr., Nicky Hilton, Mel Tormé and journalist Jim Bacon … to name a few.

In 1953, *Photoplay* named Marilyn Monroe the "Fastest Rising Star of 1952." Wearing a gold lamé see-through gown that had literally been stitched over her curves, she made a spectacular entrance. Joan Crawford told reporters, "It was the most shocking display of bad taste I have ever seen."

This type of publicity sickened DiMaggio, too. He refused to accompany her to such functions because she embarrassed him. Joe was, however, waiting for her in the darkness of the night after the award dinner.

Marilyn said she married DiMaggio "because we can't live without each other." But she accused him of physical abuse and began seeing a psychiatrist. After their divorce, Marilyn and Joe saw each other frequently in private. She told friends he was well endowed and a great lover.

"Nobody ever got cancer from sex," she said. "I like to make men happy—to see them smile." Recalling her days as a call girl, Marilyn said the compliments she received gave her confidence and "something to live for." In later years she looked upon sex as a bond of friendship. Marilyn very rarely, if ever, achieved the ultimate orgasm. She was proud of her body and preferred the freedom of nudity irrelevant to sex. She was a playful puppy. Earthy and curious. Honest and trusting.

Marilyn may go down in history as the only movie actress of her magnitude who admitted she used the casting couch to further her career. "It was part of the job," she explained. "They weren't shooting all those sexy movies just to sell peanut butter. They wanted to sample the merchandise. If you didn't go along, there were twenty-five girls who would."

Marilyn was having a discreet affair with Marlon Brando and disappearing on weekends with Joe DiMaggio when she fell in love with a playwright. "The greatest thrill of my life was at a cocktail party when my hand accidentally brushed Arthur Miller's ankle," she said.

Miller was everything Monroe hoped to find in a husband, but living with a writer was difficult for her. "He won't go anywhere," she said. "He's got to write, write, write!" Like the DiMaggio union, it was a strong sexual attraction that held this marriage together for almost five years.

Ironically it was Miller who suggested French actor Yves Montand for Marilyn's leading man in 1960. She noticed a strong resemblance to Joe DiMaggio and was fascinated to find out Montand was actually Italian. He co-starred with Marilyn in *Let's Make Love*, and brought the title to life at the Beverly Hills Hotel in Hollywood. When Yves returned to France, a heartbroken Marilyn was in no mood to film Arthur's screenplay *The Misfits*. The Millers fought bitterly over the script and were barely speaking on location in Reno.

Marilyn had a nervous breakdown and was rushed to a hospital in Los Angeles. It seemed unlikely that she would be well enough to complete *The Misfits*. But after a visit from Joe DiMaggio, her recovery was remarkable.

When the movie was finished so was Marilyn's marriage, but she was more upset over Clark Gable's fatal heart attack in November 1960. Rumors that her tardiness during production of *The Misfits* killed her idol prompted Marilyn to attempt suicide again.

There was a missing link in the breakup of Marilyn's marriages—Senator John F. Kennedy, who asked his brother-in-law Peter Lawford to arrange an introduction to the sex goddess in 1954. Marilyn met Kennedy when she was Mrs. Joe DiMaggio, and the affair blossomed during her marriage to Miller.

Marilyn maintained an apartment in New York, but bought a house in Hollywood to concentrate on her career. Though she was getting $100,000 for each film, Fox would eventually pay Elizabeth Taylor $1 million to do *Cleopatra*. But this was not the only reason Marilyn chose to be in California. She wanted to be with President John F. Kennedy who frequently stayed at

Lawford's beach house in Malibu.

Marilyn had flings with other men, but she favored Kennedy despite his lack of foreplay and hasty lovemaking. The affair was well known in Hollywood and Washington, but it was not gossip or the press that threatened this romance. It was Teamster boss Jimmy Hoffa's tape recorded proof.

Attorney General Bobby Kennedy was "elected" to tell Marilyn that she could not see his brother again, but he too got involved with her in the spring of 1962. Bobby was more compassionate than John and, according to Marilyn, proposed marriage. How he planned to deal with his wife, seven children, the Pope and his political future is a puzzle because we will never know the promises he made to Marilyn. But we do know Jimmy Hoffa hated the Attorney General more than the President.

On July 20, 1962, Marilyn had her thirteenth (or fourteenth) abortion and placed one of her last phone calls to Bobby the following week at the Justice Department in Washington. Relieved that she had not changed her mind and decided to have the baby fathered most likely by John, Bobby had his private phone number changed.

Ignored by both Kennedys, the last few weeks of Marilyn's life were ones of desperation, rage, hysteria, depression and, eventually, revenge. Ten days before her death she showed Robert Slatzer a diary containing notes of her conversations with Bobby, dealing with the Bay of Pigs, the CIA's plans to assassinate Fidel Castro, John Kennedy's link to underworld boss Sam Giancana, the murder of President Ngo Dihn Diem of South Vietnam, the "possible" assassination of President Rafaél Trujillo of the Dominican Republic and U.S. involvement in the Caribbean's Murder, Inc.

Slatzer did not think Marilyn had any intention of using this explosive information. She was, however, going public about her affairs with the Kennedy brothers: "I'm tired of lies and broken promises."

On Saturday, August 4, 1962, Bobby came to Marilyn's

home and told her, once and for all, the affair was over. She became hysterical, had to be sedated and her psychiatrist, Dr. Greenson, was summoned to the house. Later that evening Marilyn was dead. There are missing pieces as to how and where, but her love for Bobby Kennedy was the beginning of the end.

A few days later, a shocked and grieving Bob Slatzer took his last stroll around Marilyn's house and accidentally came across some broken glass *outside* her bedroom window. If Dr. Greenson had broken the pane to gain access, the shattered pieces should have been on the *inside*. "I knew then," Slatzer said, "that those involved were lying. That's when I began my investigation to prove Marilyn was murdered."

Marilyn Monroe was tragedy's child. She hungered for affection and found it in bed. She needed security and sought it in the arms of many men. But Marilyn was a love addict whose craving was never quite satisfied.

She did not believe that diamonds were a girl's best friend. Nor did she care how to marry a millionaire.

Marilyn Monroe gave more happiness than she received in her brief lifetime.

She was a joy.

1

The Early Years

She was nineteen and separated from her husband. She had a cute face framed with blondish-brown hair, a peppy personality and a fetching figure. Sitting in a bar alone, she was approached by an older man who whispered in her ear, "If I can see you in the nude, it's worth fifteen bucks." She shook her head, but not very convincingly. Fifteen dollars was a lot of money for only taking off her clothes.

"Okay," she said. "But, that's all."

That was enough. When he began to undress, she cringed. "I'm only human," he panted. "You're beautiful all over! I want you, honey."

He might have forced her into it, but he didn't. He stood there with his shirt off, but hadn't removed his trousers. He was waiting for the "lady" to make up her mind.

"Not without a rubber," she said.

He ran to a nearby drug store, thinking she'd be a dope to wait for him, but when he got back to the room, she was there. When it was over, he gave her fifteen dollars and she bought a new dress.

She had no regrets. In fact, she enjoyed being with him. The sex was no big deal. She needed the money, but not desperately. What brought her back to that bar was to belong to anyone who appreciated her. She was just another girl until she took off her clothes. Then she was in command. Men worshipped her. She looked forward to their compliments more than their money. Somehow it was all worthwhile to her in an odd sort of way. She gained the self-confidence so sadly lacking in her life. She felt alive, and the men were happy.

She began taking more of an interest in her hair, makeup and clothes. After all, this was Hollywood and she wanted to model. One of her "customers" was in the movie business and told her she was special.

"But I can't act," she exclaimed.

"That's not important in this town," he said. "Do what you're doing now, but with important men who will do something for you."

She thought about the movies but continued on with modeling and shared her body with photographers. They got her picture on the cover of several magazines that were brought to the attention of 20th Century-Fox studios.

How did she get her first break in films?

"I met the right men and gave them what they wanted," Marilyn Monroe replied.

Growing up, nobody wanted her. She belonged nowhere and to no one. She had little education, no future, no name and no father. Her maternal grandmother and grandfather died in a mental institution. Her ninety-year-old mother, who is alive as of this writing, spent most of her life in a sanitarium. Marilyn never knew if she was fathered by her mother's husband or lover.

But through it all, her childhood was not the tragedy that she would have us believe. Marilyn was fortunate compared to Lucille LeSueur, who scrubbed floors, washed dishes and was beaten with a broomstick by the school's headmistress. But Lucille was a survivor who was determined to get even with every bitch and bastard who ridiculed her. As the legendary Joan Crawford, that's precisely what she did.

Joan grew up too fast, Marilyn never grew up at all.

Both women posed in the nude. Joan needed the money. Marilyn did not. Crawford paid off the blackmailers, and never admitted filming risqué vignettes. Twenty years later, the Monroe nude calendar made her a celebrity. People were not more liberal in the fifties, but they were more understanding. Joan had everything to lose in the long run. She had become a manicured woman of taste. Marilyn never rose above the busty dumb-blonde stigma. Unlike Crawford, she continued to tell pathetic and shocking stories about her childhood. Some of them varied from the original versions while others conflicted with established dates and places. Marilyn was, of course, reaching out for love and attention. By relating a deep, dark secret to a new acquaintance, she had created a trusted friendship. These sad little fibs were tearjerkers that provoked shock and elicited sympathy. The attentive listeners were honored indeed to have Marilyn tell them privileged information about herself, and they repaid her with their loyalty.

These stories have been told since Marilyn's death thirty years ago, contributing to the complexity of ascertaining her true history. It is almost impossible to untangle the twisted web of truth and fairy tales because a "Marilyn told me" confession cannot be dismissed. Writers have to be detectives and psychiatrists to compose a worthy Monroe biography.

Marilyn's maternal grandmother, Della Hogan, married Otis Monroe around the turn of the century. Their daughter Gladys (Marilyn's mother) was born in 1902. Della and Otis, who were both born mentally unstable, divorced when he was institutionalized.

In 1917 Gladys married John Baker in Los Angeles. Divorced in 1922, she allowed John to bring up their children, Hermitt and Berneice, in Kentucky. Hermitt, a sickly boy, reportedly died.

Marilyn was the daughter of Martin Edward Mortenson, a first-generation American of Norwegian parents, who married Gladys Pearl Monroe Baker on October 11, 1924, in Los Angeles.

Marilyn Monroe was born Norma Jeane Mortenson* in the charity ward of Los Angeles General Hospital at nine-thirty on the morning of June 1, 1926. Mortenson had deserted Gladys during her pregnancy, however, and she began dating C. Stanley Gifford, who many suspected was Marilyn's real father.

Marilyn's parents were never divorced. Their marriage ended when Mortenson was killed in a motorcycle accident in 1929.

Gladys went back to work at Consolidated Film Industries and left Norma Jeane with her neighbors, the Bolenders, in Hawthorne, California. She rarely saw her mother, referring to Gladys as "the lady with the red hair."

Della fawned over her granddaughter, but supposedly tried to smother Norma Jeane with a pillow when she was only thirteen months old. Marilyn swore that she recalled waking up and gasping for breath. Whether a baby barely over a year old is capable of remembering such a traumatic incident is doubtful.

The truth lies somewhere between Marilyn's blaming the nightmare for her insomnia and Della's confinement in Norwalk State Hospital when her granddaughter was thirteen months old. The Bolenders never knew what sparked the rage in Della, who banged on their front door, screaming and shouting incoherently. The police came and took her away. Nineteen days later Della had a seizure and died of a heart attack.

---

* Gladys named her daughter after actress Norma Talmadge.

Norma Jeane might have been old enough to recall struggling with a death-pillow, but she was not old enough to grieve for Della. She lived with the Bolenders for seven years. They wanted to adopt her, but Gladys had other plans. She had saved enough money to buy a small house in Hollywood for herself and Norma Jeane in 1933.

The Bolenders were very religious people who did not drink or smoke. They attended church twice a week and said grace before every meal. In her pathetic attempt to save herself, Della had been a follower of Aimee Semple McPherson, who baptized Norma Jeane. The Bolenders were satisfied that the child had been saved and took her to prayer meetings and church services regularly.

Living with her mother was quite a change for Norma Jeane. Gladys rented part of the house to a British couple who enjoyed a smoke with their cocktails. But they were well-mannered, gracious and willing to look after Norma Jeane when her mother was working or out on dates. But Gladys, like Della, could not cope with the ups and downs of life no matter how trivial. A year after Norma Jeane moved to her mother's house, Gladys lost control for no particular reason and was admitted to Norwalk State Hospital, where Della had died. Gladys did not want anyone to adopt her daughter. Instead, she appointed her best friend, Grace McKee, to be Norma Jeane's guardian. Grace had no choice. She took the little girl to the Los Angeles Orphans' Home in 1935 and came to visit her once a week. It was difficult for Grace to bear Norma Jeane's pathetic cry, "But I'm not an orphan!"

However, the orphanage was not the horrid place that Marilyn described. The rooms were clean and airy, the food was nourishing and there was a swimming pool on the grounds. The children were paid five cents a week for doing extra chores, but hardly the task of washing one hundred dishes three times a day and scrubbing bathrooms as Marilyn later claimed.

It was difficult for Norma Jeane to understand why she had to live at the orphanage. She knew that several families, including the Bolenders, wanted to adopt her. Grace McKee was planning to marry a younger man with three children, and felt that Gladys's eleven-year-old daughter might be a burden. She could not, however, simply ignore the pleas of Norma Jeane to take her out of the orphanage.

Grace tried to please everyone. She married Erwin "Doc" Goddard, settled in Van Nuys, and placed Norma Jeane in two foster homes before welcoming her into the Goddard household. Norma Jeane got along well with the other children—Beebe, Josephine and John (Fritz), and became very close to Grace's aunt, Ana Lower, who Marilyn cherished. "Aunt Ana was the first person I ever loved," she said. "And she loved me."

Norma Jeane lived with the Goddards until she was married at the age of sixteen. Her husband, James Dougherty, said she was a virgin. Marilyn swore she had been mistreated and/or raped by a man. She had several versions of what happened and when: the man fondled her, but nothing more; she was raped, but no one believed her; he went all the way and she enjoyed it. Yet another version is that she became pregnant at fourteen and put the baby boy up for adoption when it was a few days old, but this is untrue.

What might be true is Marilyn's tale about "Doc" Goddard getting drunk one night, coming into her bedroom and giving her a "French" kiss. He never bothered her again, but she stayed away from "Doc" when he was drinking. Some Monroe historians theorize that Marilyn elaborated on this one episode, building it up into a childhood horror story. Others believe that a man pulled down Norma Jeane's panties halfway and fondled her. This version is more accepted, and a good foundation for Marilyn's vivid imagination to expand upon.

Her psychiatrist, Dr. Greenson, told author Anthony Summers that Marilyn had a "mistreatment fantasy." This malfunction had led to much speculation particularly regarding her having a baby and either giving it up or sending money to a couple who were caring for the child. To one friend she claimed it was born in her early teens. To another friend, Marilyn said she gave birth after her divorce from Dougherty.

The only person who could establish the truth is Grace McKee, who supposedly saw Norma Jeane through the pregnancy and forced her to give up the baby. But Grace committed suicide in 1953 with an overdose of barbiturates.

Marilyn had two very sound reasons for not having a child. She did not want to ruin her figure (an old wives' tale back then), and she believed she carried the strain of insanity that ran on both sides of her mother's family. By trying to establish her ability to conceive and deliver a healthy baby, Marilyn had proven her worth as the total woman. She later told her maid, Lena Pepitone, that she was a victim of rape in her early teens. Shortly after moving in with the Goddards, Norma Jeane realized she was pregnant. Grace went with her to the hospital and insisted she give up the baby. Marilyn told this fairy tale to Pepitone when she miscarried for the second time during her marriage to Arthur Miller—"See, Lena, I *can* have a baby!"

Yet Marilyn confided to close friends that it would not be fair to bring a child into the world bcause its chances of being mentally balanced were slim.

Despite the discrepancies, Marilyn was born with three strikes against her. She was described by her school teachers as happy and energetic, and she maintained a *C* average. Norma Jeane was cooperative, friendly and well behaved. But living in an orphanage and foster homes took its toll.

Grace Goddard must be given a good deal of credit for taking in Norma Jeane when she was adjusting to a new husband and three stepchildren. She might have found a way to overrule Gladys, who would not permit her daughter to be adopted. But when "Doc" obtained a good job in West Virginia, the Goddards decided to relocate. Grace knew she could not take Norma Jeane, and conferred with Aunt Ana, who was too old at sixty to be responsible for an active fifteen-year-old girl.

Who came up with the idea of marriage is another mystery. There is no doubt it was arranged by the Goddards and Aunt Ana—with Gladys's blessing—but we are talking about California, not China. The chosen groom was twenty-one, a good-looking athlete, former president of his senior class and popular with the girls. In fact, he was going steady with a beauty queen.

2

Jim

Jim Dougherty's family lived near the Goddards, and Norma Jeane often hitched a ride in his Ford coupe. He was four years older than she at a stage in life when fourteen and eighteen made a big difference. But Norma Jeane was blossoming into a mature young lady and went out on casual dates with Jim. There were no other boys who came calling, but plenty who whistled and howled when Norma Jeane's breasts bounced underneath her cheap blouses as she paraded down the street. She was becoming aware of the mating call at the age of fifteen. Since the opposite sex had paid her little attention before, no one had bothered to explain the facts of life to Norma Jeane.

Jim might have been like a big brother to her at the onset, but he soon found in Norma Jeane a delightful and attentive date. Grace encouraged the "courtship" because, as she told the Doughertys, "I don't want to send her back to the orphanage when we move to West Virginia." Though Marilyn would say in later years that the Goddards abandoned her, Grace was very concerned about Norma Jeane, and if marriage was possible, she wanted to make the arrangements personally before leaving California.

Jim was not the sort of fellow who could be talked into giving up his freedom. He had a good job in an aircraft factory and all

17

the girls he wanted. Perhaps he might have waited a year or two before getting married, but he did not want Norma Jeane to go back to the orphanage, either. She was not his type, but she was a very pretty girl with a curvacious figure and a dreamy look in her eyes when she was with him.

The wedding took place on June 19, 1942, three weeks after Norma Jeane's sixteenth birthday, at the home of friends in Westwood. Grace chose this house because it had a winding staircase for the bride to make her descent. Aunt Ana bought Norma Jeane's wedding gown and gave her away. The Bolenders attended the wedding, but Gladys had a setback and could not be there. The Goddards sent their best wishes from West Virginia.

The only mishap of the day was at the wedding reception in the Florentino Gardens when a waiter spilled tomato sauce on the groom's rented white tuxedo jacket. There was no honeymoon because Jim had to work on Monday.

Though Dougherty admits his marriage to Norma Jeane was arranged, he said they were happy and very compatible sexually. Her cooking left a lot to be desired. She gave him raw fish and put salt in his coffee by mistake. One night she served only peas and carrots because "I like the colors." Her first attempt at making highballs for friends, she filled the glasses to the rim with liquor, emptying the bottle on the first round. Jim was patient, however. If he lost his temper, she cried for hours.

Dougherty said Norma Jeane liked sex and wanted to make love more often than he did. A few months after they were married, Jim was moved to the night shift. A romantic Norma Jeane put passionate love notes in his lunch pail that often embarrassed him, but certainly impressed his co-workers.

At the outbreak of World War II, Jim joined the Maritime Service and they moved to Catalina Island, where he was a physical instructor. Norma Jeane, who was one of the few women on Catalina at that time, became the center of attention when she went out for a walk. Dougherty was proud of his wife, but thought she might tone down her makeup, lengthen her dresses and wear looser sweaters. Still, she had an innocence that was refreshing. Their sex had diminished when Jim was on the night shift, but it was better than ever on Catalina. Norma Jeane paraded herself for the other servicemen, but remained loyal to Dougherty, who was father, brother, lover and husband to her.

In 1944, Jim was sent overseas to Australia. Norma Jeane lived with the Doughertys and worked in a defense plant packing and inspecting parachutes. She was frustrated and lonely without Jim. It was during their first separation that both realized how much they meant to each other. When he came home on furlough a few months later, Norma Jeane ran into his arms at the station. At her urging, they headed for a motel and spent the next few days in bed. Norma Jeane had brought along a new sheer black nightie for her husband's homecoming. She clung to him for three weeks, dreading his leaving her. Jim sensed this, but there was a war going on and he was shipped out to the Pacific.

Norma Jeane returned to her dull routine at the plant until *Yank* magazine assigned photographer David Conover to take pictures of women working in defense plants. When he spotted Norma Jeane, Conover asked the foreman if she could be his model for three days. He was very impressed with the pictures and offered her more modeling jobs. Norma Jeane's photos came to the attention of the Blue Book Model Agency, and her new career was launched. She worked at the defense plant, calling in sick if a modeling job came along, and attended charm school at night. Norma Jeane seldom saw the Doughertys, who took a dim view of her new life-style. To avoid a confrontation with them, she moved in with Aunt Ana Lower.

Jim had not been receiving many letters from his wife compared to the usual stack waiting for him in every port. She finally got around to writing him about her work as a model and living with Aunt Ana. He was not disturbed or suspicious. If Jim suspected his wife did not want their marriage to last or that she was running around with other men, he never said so. He was sure everything would be all right when he came home to stay.

When the Goddards moved back to California in 1946, they were informed that Gladys was well enough to leave the hospital if she had a permanent residence. Grace was glad to have her. Norma Jeane became reacquainted with her mother and suggested they share a small apartment at Aunt Ana's. But Gladys was agitated over her daughter's frequent out-of-town modeling assignments and the men who kept her out all night. Norma Jeane did as she pleased, and a nervous Gladys checked herself back into the sanitarium.

Jim came home for a cozy but brief reunion with his wife. He didn't like her bleached hair or her busy schedule. But what bothered him most were the unpaid bills. What had she done with his allotment checks? Well, a model needs pretty clothes. Jim had saved his money to take Norma Jeane to a swank nightclub, but he used the three hundred dollars to pay bills. Whatever was left over, she needed for makeup, and maybe, a down payment on a used car. When Jim went back to sea this time, he was less confident about his marriage. And he was angry at himself for not being firm with his wife about money.

It appears that Jim did not suspect Norma Jeane was having affairs with other men. Possibly, he did not want to think about it because she couldn't get enough of him in bed. Was it sex or love that made her the aggressor?

Norma Jeane was very serious about her modeling career and getting by on her merits until she was sent on assignment with a young Hungarian photographer, André de Dienes. They took an extensive car trip to suitable locations from Oregon to the Mojave. He wanted her to pose in the nude. She didn't think so. He tried to seduce her to no avail. They had separate rooms in motels until a blizzard forced them to spend the night in the only room available. Dienes had been impressed with the sweet and wholesome nineteen-year-old from the beginning, but after they were intimate, he wanted to marry her. He knew that she was not happily married and this was confirmed by Aunt Ana when he was invited for dinner. By the time he and Norma Jeane returned to Los Angeles, they were in love. Marilyn said in later years that Dienes was the only man she had gone to bed with besides Dougherty. But the thirty-two-year-old Dienes was a sophisticated lover who astonished (and excited) Norma Jeane with a variety of sexual variations.

Before shipping out to the Orient, Jim came home, but he saw very little of his wife who was busy with her modeling assignments. She talked about nothing else except her work and how much she wanted to get into the movies. Eventually Dougherty confronted Norma Jeane and gave her a choice—career or marriage. She did not respond.

In the spring of 1946, Jim was in China when he received divorce papers from Las Vegas. Dougherty was deeply hurt. When he got over the shock, his concern was for Norma Jeane and what would become of her. She had second thoughts, too, but one goal in particular prevented her from turning back—the movies.

Dienes was working in New York and keeping in touch with Norma Jeane. He assumed they would be married, but when he returned to Hollywood, Dienes caught her with another man.

Emmeline Snively, head of the Blue Book Model Agency, was grooming Norma Jeane for a screen test. Thus, the urgent trip to Las Vegas for a divorce. Meanwhile, Snively arranged for her protégée to grace the covers of *Laff, Peek and See*, and *U.S. Camera*.

In July 1946, the *Los Angeles Times* ran a brief item about Howard Hughes, who was recuperating from injuries sustained from a plane crash. Looking through magazines, he was attracted to a cover girl by the name of Norma Jeane Dougherty, and told an aide to offer her a movie contract.

Hughes would have a fling with her later on, but in the

meantime, a bit of gossip linking her with the tycoon, who discovered Jean Harlow and Jane Russell, paid off with a call from 20th Century-Fox.

Jim Dougherty, home on leave in the summer of 1946, drove Norma Jeane to Fox for the screen test. He had called her about a pile of bills and parking tickets that she chose to ignore. Jim got the impression Norma Jeane was barely getting by financially even though she was making decent money as a model and living with Aunt Ana.

Precisely when Norma Jeane became a call girl is not certain. In later years, Marilyn was vague. Her tale about hanging out in bars after Jim went overseas has some discrepancies. But her version relating to the need for money while waiting for a break in films has credence.

3

Marilyn

Ben Lyon was the casting director at 20th Century-Fox. Married to actress Bebe Daniels, Lyon had been a popular star in the twenties. One of his more noted films was Howard Hughes's *Hell's Angels*. After serving in the RAF during the war, he became a British talent scout for 20th Century-Fox and eventually ended up in Hollywood as a casting director. Lyon was a good-looking forty-five when Norma Jeane Dougherty was ushered into his office.

Lyon recalled she was wearing a simple flowered dress and her golden blonde hair was shoulder length. What impressed him most (aside from her figure) was Norma Jeane's lovely skin that he described as "peaches and cream." Lyon arranged a screen test for her in color two days later. She did not have any dialogue because Lyon wanted to emphasize her physical attributes. Wearing a sequined gown, Norma Jeane was filmed from every angle—walking away from the camera, sitting down and walking toward the camera.

Darryl Zanuck, head of Fox, viewed the screen test and said, "Sign her up!" When Lyon told Norma Jeane, she broke down and wept. He then explained that the studio contract system had many thorns among the roses. She would start out at $75 a week. If her six-month option was picked up, she would earn

$100, and so on up to $1500 a week in the seventh year. Norma Jeane was now the property of 20th Century-Fox. She was so thrilled and grateful that it never occurred to her what it meant to be a commodity, a piece of merchandise. She could have made more money as a model, but her desire to be somebody—illuminated on the big screen—became an obsession. The day Norma Jeane signed her contract she told a friend, "I've sucked my last cock!" (She said this on other rewarding occasions.)

Ben Lyon took it upon himself to change Norma Jeane's name almost immediately. They tried Jean Norman and Carole Lind, but Lyon wasn't satisfied. Then one day it came to him. "You remind me of Marilyn Miller!" he exclaimed.

"Who's she?" Norma Jeane asked.

"A beautiful star of Broadway musicals. She's dead now, but there's an amazing resemblance. You're a Marilyn!"

"I am?"

"No question, but we need a last name."

"How about Monroe? That was my grandmother's name."

Lyon beamed. "Marilyn Monroe ... Marilyn Monroe. It glides off the tongue with ease. Perfect."

Norma Jeane Mortenson Dougherty no longer existed. The past was behind her—or so she thought. As Marilyn Monroe, she reported to the studio every day for acting lessons and to pose endlessly for pin-up pictures. She hung around the publicity department at Fox and was not overlooked by press photographers or reporters on the lot.

Marilyn went after bigger game, but could not get in to see Darryl Zanuck. She recognized Fox mogul Joseph M. Schenck leaving the studio in his limousine and gave him her cover-girl smile. He told his driver to stop, motioned to Marilyn and wanted to know her name. When Schenck found out she was under contract, he gave Marilyn his card and said, "Give me a call and we'll have dinner."

Joe Schenck was a very powerful man in Hollywood, but he was no Sir Lancelot. Approaching seventy, he was stocky, bald and chubby. Schenck was born in Russia and emigrated to the United States in 1893. After succeeding in the drugstore business, Joe ventured into amusement parks, one of which was purchased by Marcus Loew, who convinced Schenck to become partners in a chain of theaters, Consolidated Enterprises. In 1917 he gained recognition as the producer of Fatty Arbuckle and Buster Keaton films. Joe was married to actress Norma Talmadge when he became chairman of the board of United Artists in 1924. Three years later he established 20th Century Productions, and in 1935 merged with Fox Film Corporation. Joe was forced to resign as president of 20th Century-Fox Corp. in 1941 after being convicted of income tax evasion and sent to the U.S. Correction Institute in Danbury, Connecticut. Four months later President Truman gave Schenck a full pardon when he testified for the government about annual bribes of $50,000 to union racketeers. Studio heads, guilty of the same charges, had mixed feelings about Schenck after he returned to Hollywood. When he met Marilyn, Joe was an executive producer at Fox and working at his leisure.

In 1934, Norma Talmadge divorced Schenck to marry comedian George Jessel. In Europe, Joe met the exotic Merle Oberon, who became his mistress. He lavished her with furs and diamonds, but by the time Joe got around to proposing marriage, Merle was involved with Leslie Howard.

Schenck did not remarry. The women he had loved were a disappointment to him in the end, but he was not a bitter man. Instead he found great pleasure in surrounding himself with beautiful young girls at open-house buffets on Sunday at his luxurious estate in Holmby Hills. Whether Marilyn visited Schenck alone or with others, she was picked up and driven home in a limousine.

Marilyn and Joe developed a sincere friendship. She was

mesmerized by his Hollywood stories, listening late into the night and often sleeping in the guest house. At the age of seventy, Schenck was not active sexually. His doctor gave him shots that induced erections, but they did not last long. Marilyn said Joe liked to look at her in the nude and fondle her breasts. If she "serviced" him, Marilyn was not rewarded.

They saw each other on a regular basis, but she did not discuss her career with him nor did he ask. Marilyn was thrilled to get her first role at Fox, *Scudda Hoo! Scudda Hay!* Most of her scenes in a rowboat were cut out, however. What is left of Marilyn at a distance cannot be recognized.

Columnist Sheila Graham claimed Ben Lyon was having an affair with Marilyn before and after she signed with Fox. Then she pleaded with Lyon to get her into a picture and he did, but Marilyn was disappointed when she ended up on the cutting-room floor. Whether Ben wanted to continue his affair with Marilyn or thought his wife was suspicious, he stuck out his neck again and got Marilyn in *Dangerous Years*. She played a waitress in a teenage hangout and had a few lines.

Ben Lyon, however, had the sad task of telling Marilyn that her one year's option was not going to be renewed. She broke down in tears. Lyon said he had no idea why Zanuck dropped her. No one did. There were rumors about her sleeping around with the top brass at Fox and they were tired of her. Zanuck was a ladies' man, but said he wouldn't go to bed with Marilyn if she paid him. As for Schenck, he knew nothing about it.

Marilyn barely made a living modeling and barhopping. "I lived on thirty cents a day and couldn't afford a place to live," she said.

Marilyn drifted from bed to bed. Two mattresses she shared belonged to the Chaplin brothers, Charlie, Jr., and Sydney. The boys' lives might be considered typical of Hollywood offspring, being sent away to school and growing up trying to find themselves. Their mother, Lita Grey, was a child bride of Charlie, Sr., but the marriage had lasted a brief and stormy three years.

Marilyn had an affair with the twenty-one-year-old Charlie, Jr., who was just getting by on his meager allowance. Author Anthony Summers (*Goddess*) wrote that Marilyn became pregnant by Charlie and had one of her first abortions. Though they remained friends, the affair ended when Chaplin found Marilyn in bed with brother Sydney. (Charlie, Jr., became an alcoholic and died at the age of 42.)

Without a place to live, Marilyn carried her belongings around with her in late 1947. One might ask, "Where was Joe Schenck?" She went to his Sunday buffets for something to eat and occasionally met with him privately for a square meal. Marilyn finally told him about Fox not renewing her contract. He was encouraging—"Don't give up" or "Don't worry about it," he'd say—but Joe did not pick up a telephone. Though Marilyn was known in Hollywood as Schenck's mistress, this was not the case. It was an exchange of champagne dinners and fellatio. Marilyn was at the lowest ebb of her life, but she managed to be cheerful with Joe and patient with him sexually. "Sometimes it took hours," she related to a friend. "I was relieved when he fell asleep!"

In December of 1947, Marilyn, broke and unhappy, struck up a conversation with handsome screen baritone John Carroll at a drive-in restaurant. He took her home to his wife, Lucille Ryman, an MGM talent scout. They offered Marilyn the use of a spare bedroom in their apartment.

The six-foot-four Carroll was at one time considered by MGM mogul Louis B. Mayer to be another Clark Gable. In 1936 John married his leading lady in *Hi, Gaucho*, Hungarian-born Steffi Duna. They had a daughter, Juliana, before their divorce in in 1942. Carroll appeared with Joan Crawford in *Susan and God*, with Eleanor Powell in *Lady Be Good*, with Abbott and Costello in *Rio Rita*, with John Wayne in *Flying Tigers*, and in *Fiesta* with Esther Williams.

In 1942, John Carroll and Susan Hayward fell in love. She

was warned that he was a con man—and broke. Susan found out for herself when Carroll told her to pick out a diamond ring and send him the bill. He objected to the price and she broke the engagement.

After his marriage to Lucille Ryman and around the time he became involved with Marilyn, John's all-nude party was exposed in *Confidential* magazine. Later on he was sued by a seventy-year-old widow who demanded the return of $228,000. John insisted it was half that amount and beside she had given it to him. He was in and out of court until the case was settled quietly.

Aside from a luxurious apartment in West Hollywood, the Carrolls owned a ranch in the San Fernando Valley. Obviously Lucille had the money in the family, but she was a bright MGM executive who saw potential in Marilyn, and signed her to a three-month contract. The Carrolls gave her board, room, spending money and acting and singing lessons. Marilyn and John became lovers, and she wanted to marry him. Lucille said that was all right with her, but it wasn't all right with John. This was a simple case of Marilyn's ignorance of how to play the Hollywood game. She would never learn. There was an innocence to her gullibility that gave people the impression she was not very bright.

Lucille Ryman knew the score *and* her husband well. Marilyn was back on the street again, but two years later, Ryman would prove there were no hard feelings.

4

Fred

In early 1948, Joe Schenck finally made his move. He asked Harry Cohn, head of Columbia Pictures, to give Marilyn a six-month contract. Cohn said, "If it's that important to you, Joe, I'll do it." Marilyn signed for $75 a week in March, 1948, and was put to work in the low-budget musical *Ladies of the Chorus*.

Columbia's makeup experts raised Marilyn's forehead slightly, removing the excess hair first by hot wax and later by electrolysis. Columnist Sheila Graham wrote, "Marilyn's new wide brow transformed her from being merely attractive into a beauty. There was fine, downy, blonde hair all over her face, which, although covered with makeup, gave a luminous quality to her skin on the screen. She would spend hours experimenting with makeup—putting it on, taking it off. Her eyelashes, half an inch long, were completely white and had to be dyed."

Marilyn would eventually have her protruding teeth corrected, her nose and chin reconstructed and her baby-fine hair dyed platinum. What little Harry Cohn had done to improve Marilyn's appearance was commendable since he had no intention of signing her to a long-term contract. The biggest S.O.B. in town, he had a foul mouth and nasty disposition.

When Cohn died in 1958, thousands went to his funeral. The joke going around Hollywood was that everyone attended to make sure he was really dead.

Obviously Joe had something on Harry, but once he kept his part of the bargain, Cohn tried to seduce the girl he assumed was Schenck's mistress. "Harry just told you to get into bed without saying hello," Marilyn said. Though she denied finding this out personally, those who remember her in 1948 think she was desperate enough to go through with it.

Marilyn was at Columbia for only a short time, but she met two people at the studio who would have a great deal of influence over her for many years—vocal coach, Fred Karger, and drama coach, Natasha Lytess.

Karger was ten years older than Marilyn, good-looking, clean-cut, talented and recently divorced. For her it was love at first sight. Karger thought of Marilyn as just another starlet who was expected to carry a tune in a second-rate musical. In the process he took pity on her because she could not always afford to eat and he invited her home for dinner. Fred was living with a six-year-old son, his mother, divorced sister and her children. The Karger family became very fond of Marilyn. When they found out she was living in a dingy furnished room, Mrs. Karger invited her to stay with them for a while.

Marilyn and Fred became lovers, but he was never serious about her. She was mad about Karger and wanted to marry him. He responded in bed, but was reluctant to take her out in public because Marilyn gave the impression of being a trollop. Her clothes were all wrong. She wore cheap low-cut dresses that attracted the wrong kind of attention. He blamed her love for him on her inability to separate the bedroom from the drawing room. Marilyn chased him, nonetheless, and proposed marriage. Karger said that was out of the question because she was not fit to be his son's stepmother.

But nothing could diminish Marilyn's love for Fred. For Christmas in 1948 she bought him a $500 gold watch that took her several years to pay off and by the time she had he was married to Jane Wyman (November 1952). They eventually divorced two years later and remarried in 1961. Ironically, Karger died on August 5, 1979, seventeen years to the day of Marilyn's death.

Ladies of the Chorus was a forgettable film about the ups and downs of being a hoofer. Marilyn sang "Every Baby Needs a Da-Da-Daddy" and "Anyone Can Tell I Love You." Few critics bothered to review the movie, but *Motion Picture Herald* wrote, "One of the bright spots is Miss Monroe's singing. She is pretty and with her pleasing voice and style, she shows promise."

Harry Cohn did not agree and dropped Marilyn. "I bet she never gets anywhere," he said.

Many of Marilyn's friends believe Fred Karger was the love of her life. Yet she had affairs with other men during her relationship with him. Milton Berle claims he was intimate with Marilyn while she was filming *Ladies of the Chorus*. Orson Welles had a "dressing room" fling with her shortly after his divorce from Rita Hayworth. Then there was Howard Hughes, who had recently acquired RKO Studios.

Journalist James Bacon met Marilyn at a party in early 1949 and offered to drive her home.

"Where do you live?" he asked.

"Joe Schenck's guest house," she replied.

Bacon described the estate as being "so big that even the rooms had rooms." Marilyn invited him to the guest house, which was stocked with Dom Pérignon. She told Jim about her bad luck at Columbia. "Harry [Cohn] called me a goddamn cunt and said he never wanted to see me again," she said.

Bacon opened another bottle of champagne and before long he and Marilyn were in bed. As they were about to make love, she got an urgent call from Schenck. In retrospect, Bacon thought the incident was rather funny. "With agonizing slowness, she started combing her hair and putting on makeup," he said. "Somehow I felt sorry for poor Joe, sitting up in his master bedroom counting the seconds until that stiff cock started drooping."

On her way out the door Marilyn turned to Bacon and smiled, "This won't take long." Within a few minutes she was back with a giggle—"Late again!"

Bacon's intimacy with Marilyn lasted until 1951. She wanted to go out on New Year's Eve and did not have a date.

He apologized for having other plans with his wife. "I don't think she would understand," he told Marilyn, who was always friendly to Bacon after that, but the romance was over.

Nineteen forty-eight and 1949 were bewildering years for Marilyn. She had been dropped by two studios, Aunt Ana died, and Jim Dougherty remarried. She was trying to get over Fred Karger and had walked out on him many times, but always returned. When she wasn't living with him, Marilyn stayed with Natasha Lytess, who lived across the street, or in Joe Schenck's guest house.

Marilyn said in later years that she had more than one abortion during her fervent affair with Karger. Once again we have to take her word for it. Possibly she was faithful to him for a little while. Otherwise how could Marilyn possibly know whose baby she aborted unless she fantasized that he was the real father?

Friend Pat Newcomb made a very interesting statement some years later: "Marilyn Monroe never told anybody everything."

Natasaha Lytess had studied and worked with the great Austrian director Max Reinhardt in Europe. She fled to the United States as a refugee in the 1930s with her Jewish lover, writer Bruno Frank, and settled in Beverly Hills with their daughter, Barbara. They mingled with other European intellectuals such as directors Preston Sturges, William

Dieterle and Ernst Lubitsch. When Frank died in 1945, Natasha found work as a diction coach at Columbia Pictures, and advanced quickly to head of the drama department. She was a thin, unattractive woman with gray hair and piercing eyes—a serious person who did not go out of her way to be congenial.

Natasha was assigned to improve Marilyn's diction for *Ladies of the Chorus*. She was appalled when the blonde starlet walked into her office wearing a clinging red low-cut knit dress without a bra. Marilyn spoke with a nervous squeaky voice and had a blank expression on her face. But she admitted her shortcomings and wanted to learn. If Marilyn had shown an ounce of cockiness, Natasha would not have been as cooperative. Their friendship endured because Natasha's apartment was the perfect retreat for Marilyn between bouts with Fred. Eventually she moved in with Natasha.

Marilyn's next appearance on the screen was brief—in fact, less than a minute. Groucho Marx was making *Love Happy* at United Artists, and looking for a sexy blonde "dish" who wiggles up to him and says, "Some men are following me." He takes one look at her with raised eyebrows and replies, "I can't imagine why."

Marilyn concentrated on her walk, supposedly cutting a quarter of an inch off one of her high heels. The result was a unique wiggle that became a trademark. Groucho tried to bed her down, but she ignored his advances. Producer Lester Cowan thought Marilyn was a super gimmick and sent her on tour to promote *Love Happy*. She was interviewed by Louella Parsons and Earl Wilson, but Monroe was totally unprepared and not considered newsworthy. Aside from seeing New York City for the first time, she had accomplished nothing.

Marilyn was flat broke when she returned to Los Angeles. Finding someone to buy her a meal was not difficult, but when she could not come up with fifty dollars, the finance company repossessed her 1941 Pontiac. Without a car, she was out of business.

In desperation, Marilyn called photographer Tom Kelley. She had done beer ads for him and he asked her frequently to model nude for him. She was afraid the pictures would get into the wrong hands and declined. But now it was a matter of survival. Tom assured Marilyn her face would not be recognizable and that his wife Natalie would be present.

On May 27, 1949, Kelley spread out a large piece of red velvet, and Marilyn Monroe posed for what would become one of the most famous nude calendars of all time. Tom paid her fifty dollars and she got her car back.

Marilyn got a small part as a chorine in *A Ticket to Tomahawk*, a satirical Western with Dan Dailey and Anne Baxter at 20th Century-Fox. The film received excellent reviews. The Colorado scenery was magnificent, the plot was good and Dan Dailey was superb. Watching the film today, one's eyes are on Marilyn, but when *A Ticket to Tomahawk* opened in May of 1950, no one paid attention to her.

The month before, however, she exuded enough sex for thirty seconds in *Love Happy* to attract an agent who had the right connections. He recalled meeting her poolside at the Racquet Club in Palm Springs. Their brief conversation had to do with his predicting she would be a big star one day. Marilyn had heard that one before and ignored it. At the time, she was in love with tall, dark and handsome John Carroll, who towered over the balding midget of an agent who represented William Morris, the most powerful theatrical agency in the world.

The little man, whose nose came up to Marilyn's nipples, invited her for lunch. She was not at her best and didn't care. Besides her money problems and lagging career, Marilyn was carrying a torch for Fred Karger. If they were still intimate, he had made it very clear that marriage was out of the question. She wasn't good enough for him, and she didn't have what it took to be in movies. Never good enough for anybody or anything. This was the story of her life, she told the little man.

He didn't think so. . . .

5

Johnny

Johnny Hyde was fifty-three years old when he met Marilyn. A mere five-foot-three, he still seemed to tower over his fellow agents and the Hollywood greats he represented—John Huston, Lana Turner, Rita Hayworth, Bob Hope and Al Jolson.

A native of Russia, he had come to the United States with his mother and father, who were circus performers. Johnny changed his last name from Haidabura to Hyde, and went to work in the Loew vaudeville booking office. When he was twenty-one, he joined the William Morris Agency and rose to the top quickly. Johnny was a master at handling and promoting talent. He was well liked by his clients and respected by the studio moguls with whom he negotiated. Johnny was tough, but fair. He took a personal interest in the people he represented and was as devoted to their welfare as he was to the all-mighty dollar on their contracts.

Johnny was a married millionaire with children. He had everything except a healthy heart. That did not slow him down, but he watched his diet and drank sparingly. Though Johnny was not linked publicly with other women, he had his share of them before his heart condition worsened. Mrs. Hyde apparently looked the other way as all professional Hollywood wives are expected to do if they want their marriages to last.

Marilyn's drive and determination was dwindling when she met Johnny Hyde. Her life was in such disarray, she was struggling to free herself from Karger once and for all. Having no one else to confide in, Marilyn opened up her heart to Hyde and he listened. Whatever encouragement he gave about her career, she couldn't grasp right away. So Marilyn talked about Fred until she got it (not him) out of her system. Johnny absorbed every word she said, but he was studying her at the same time. Hyde noticed a small bump on the tip of Marilyn's nose and the fact that she had no chin. Her hairline had not been raised enough and she needed more work done on her teeth. These were minor flaws, but Johnny was willing to absorb whatever it cost to correct them. There was never any doubt in his mind that Marilyn should be a platinum blonde, and he made regular appointments for her at the best hairdressers in Beverly Hills.

Hyde bought her a new wardrobe of chic dresses, gowns and accessories, escorted her to nightclubs and elite dinner parties. Natasha disliked Johnny intensely. She did not approve of Marilyn's jeopardizing her reputation by running around blatantly with a married man who was turning her into a Hollywood freak rather than a serious actress.

Hyde was obsessed with the Monroe image he diligently created, and within months he was deeply in love with her. After twenty years of marriage he left his beautiful wife, former actress Mozelle Cravens, and their four sons. Mrs. Hyde filed for divorce, and Johnny bought a mansion on North Palm Drive in Beverly Hills. When Marilyn moved in with him, she had a bitter argument with Natasha.

Johnny's first attempt at getting her a juicy movie role was in *The Asphalt Jungle*. His client John Huston was directing the picture and agreed to test Marilyn for the part of Louis Calhern's mistress, Angela.

James Bacon was leaving the Thalberg Building at MGM just as she was arriving for the screen test. "Marilyn, what the hell have you done to yourself?" he asked. "You look grotesque. You look like a filing cabinet with the top drawer pulled out."

"They're looking for a girl with big bazoons," she said.

A few days later Bacon asked Huston what happened. "Well," John said, "I reached into her sweater, pulled out the falsies and said, 'You've got the part, Marilyn.' "

Huston had no choice according to author Sandra Shevey. Hyde's friend Lucille Ryman virtually blackmailed Huston into using Marilyn, since he had stabled his horses at Ryman's ranch without being charged for years, and wanted to continue the arrangement.

In *The Asphalt Jungle* Marilyn proved she possessed more than a big bust and swaying fanny. The *New York Times* did not mention her name, but raved about the film and everyone in it. *Photoplay* said, "There's a beautiful blonde, too, name of Marilyn Monroe, who plays Calhern's girl friend, and makes the most of her footage." The *New York Herald-Tribune* thought she lent "a documentary effect to a lurid exposition." Marilyn said in later years, "Personally, I think the best performance I ever gave was in *The Asphalt Jungle*."

Johnny was sure MGM would sign her to a contract, but Dore Schary, head of production, did not think Marilyn was star material or that she had the class and talent befitting a member of the MGM family.

Marilyn had a small part in *The Fireball*, with Mickey Rooney, at 20th Century-Fox, where Johnny Hyde negotiated an unusual deal with her former boss, Darryl Zanuck—a one-week guaranteed contract for *All About Eve*, with a seven-year option starting at $500 a week. Marilyn would be playing with pros in this ultra-sophisticated film about the New York theater: Bette Davis as the aging Broadway actress, George Sanders in the role of theatrical critic Addison de Witt, Anne Baxter as the scheming Eve, and Celeste Holm as the wife of playwright Hugh Marlowe.

Marilyn plays the sexy ingenue "sponsored" by George Sanders with whom she shared her two scenes. She is introduced by him as "a graduate of the Copacabana School of Dramatic Arts" in *All About Eve*. Sanders, who had met Marilyn at a party a few months previously, fell in love with her instantly and proposed marriage. Though he was slightly drunk and his wife Zsa Zsa Gabor was there, George did not hide his feelings. Working with Marilyn gave him another chance to warm up to her until Zsa Zsa found out and forbade him to have lunch with Marilyn. George did, however, spend most of his time with her on the set because she was terrified of Bette Davis. The other members of the cast were nervous, too, but had enough experience to deal with her. Marilyn, however, threw up before and after her scenes with Bette.

Sanders told author Lawrence Quirk that Davis whispered to him within Marilyn's hearing, "That little blonde slut can't act her way out of a paper bag! She thinks if she wiggles her ass and coos away, she can carry her scene—well, she can't!" Quirk wrote that Davis let Marilyn have it to her face: "I know and you know and everyone knows that kitten voice of yours is goddamned lousy—and it's lousy because you never trained it as a real actress does—a shame you never had stage training." Marilyn managed to hold back the tears (and her erupting stomach) until she was off the movie set.

In defense of Davis, she was snarling and sarcastic even to her friends. It was her nature to rant and rave even under the best of circumstances. As for Marilyn, she was an hour late on several occasions, flubbed her lines and had to repeat the same scene twenty-five times.

Shortly before she died, Bette Davis told Larry King on his CNN talk show that she saw something in Marilyn and knew she would be a big star someday, but that others associated with *All About Eve* did not agree.

(The first time a young and giggly Linda Evans worked with Barbara Stanwyck, she did not know her lines and made the mistake of bending over. Barbara gave her a swift kick in the pants!)

Marilyn may have benefited from Bette's tongue-lashing because she delivered her few lines of clever dialogue very well. They were directed at Sanders whose character was indestructible, but Marilyn put him down with perfect voice inflections.

All About Eve received fourteen Academy Award nominations, but won only four major awards—Joe Mankiewicz for Best Director and Best Screenplay, the Oscar for Best Picture, and George Sanders for Best Supporting Actor. (Davis lost to Judy Holliday in *Born Yesterday* for Best Actress.)

Bette Davis said one of her biggest disappointments was not winning an Oscar for her Margo Channing. She snubbed Sanders, who hissed in Bette's ear, "Sour grapes?" She turned around and spat at George. But not all was lost. Bette married her leading man in *All About Eve*, Gary Merrill.

Johnny Hyde had for some time begged Marilyn to marry him. She had become his whole life, extending himself to the detriment of his declining health. Maybe she should be commended for her honesty—"I love you, Johnny, but I'm not *in* love with you." On the other hand, he needed her. She might have made his last few months more comfortable and contented. Hyde was not expected to live long and wanted Marilyn to inherit the mansion and his money. It was obvious to everyone in Hollywood that he loved Marilyn deeply and had gotten a divorce to marry her. Strange as it seems, she might have gained a great deal of respect from prominent people in the movie industry if she had married Hyde. With no one to guide her, Marilyn stuck to her old-fashioned scruples. Natasha, who had the most influence over her, despised Johnny, but should have considered Marilyn's financial future under the circumstances.

Hyde wanted to provide for her. Had she married him, he most certainly would have done so, having proved himself by divorcing his wife of twenty years and decorating a home for Marilyn. To her way of thinking, it would have been obvious that she married Johnny for his money as he became weaker and less active. (Hyde's chauffeur carried him to and from the house.) His failing health was no secret in Hollywood. The consensus was that Marilyn's sexual needs were killing Johnny, but it's more likely he tried too hard to please her. Marilyn told a friend that during her lovemaking with him, she whispered, "Oh, Johnny, you're hurting me." He probably didn't believe it, but this was her way of making him feel young and virile.

At Hyde's urging, Marilyn accepted small parts in *Right Cross* and *Hometown Story* at MGM. She was having costume fittings for *As Young as You Feel* at Fox when Johnny had a heart attack and was rushed to the hospital. Marilyn remained at his bedside, and on December 18, 1950, he died. The Hyde family took possession of the mansion and told Marilyn to remove her belongings immediately. Jewelry and expensive clothes that Johnny had given her were missing, but she said nothing. Ignoring the family's request that she not attend the funeral, Marilyn made an appearance dressed in black. She threw herself across the casket, screaming Johnny's name and pleading with him to wake up. It was pathetic to some mourners while others thought she made a fool of herself.

In her grief Marilyn decided she could have saved Johnny's life if she had married him. "You're the only one who can," he told her. Marilyn never forgave herself. "He was the only person who ever really cared about me," she said in later years.

After Hyde's death, she moved back with Natasha and tried to commit suicide by taking thirty Nembutal capsules. Natasha found Marilyn just in time. "Most of the capsules were still in her mouth," Natasha said. "She was waiting for them to melt and trickle down, to destroy her life. She hadn't expected me back for several hours."

Marilyn was not included in Hyde's will. In early December 1950, Johnny told one of his attorneys that Marilyn had changed her mind about marriage, but he thought time was against him.

So Johnny decided to leave her one third of his estate, but never got around to the legalities. He died a few weeks later.

That Hyde did not provide for Marilyn earlier was partially her fault. Instead of attending the premiere of *The Asphalt Jungle* with Johnny, she went with Fred Karger. There were also numerous occasions when Hyde couldn't find her. Natasha remembered his telephone call inquiring about Marilyn's whereabouts. "I've been waiting, waiting," he told Natasha. "I've never known such selfishness."

But Hyde had secured Marilyn's future by negotiating a contract at 20th Century-Fox. If she had to choose between one third of his estate and the advancement of her career, Marilyn would have preferred the latter, anyway.

6

Mogul Carousel

Marilyn worried that Fox would not pick up her seven-year-option because Zanuck was not impressed with her. She could no longer rely on Johnny Hyde, but she still had Joe Schenck, who spoke privately with Fox president, Spyros Skouras. In January of 1951, Marilyn signed the contract for $500 a week, escalating to $1500 in seven years.

Zanuck had control over her films, however, and put Marilyn in a series of dumb-blonde roles. *As Young as You Feel* is a delightful comedy with Monty Woolley and Thelma Ritter about big business and the secretary's proper conduct with her boss. The *New York Times* wrote, "Marilyn Monroe is superb as the secretary and Constance Bennett as the neglected wife." In *Love Nest* Marilyn plays an ex-WAC living in an old New York brownstone with the likes of June Haver, William Lundigan, Frank Fay and Jack Paar.

In *Let's Make it Legal*, Marilyn flirts with Claudette Colbert's wealthy boyfriend. The *New York Daily News* said, "Marilyn Monroe is amusing in a brief role as a beautiful shapely blonde who has her eye on Zachary Scott and his millions."

These movies hold up today. Cleverly written and well acted, they are more popular now because Marilyn Monroe can be seen in them. Any of her early films are considered B classics.

During production of *As Young as You Feel* shortly after Johnny's death, Marilyn was introduced to playwright Arthur Miller on the movie set. She had been crying and he tried to cheer her up. A few days later they attended the same party and were drawn to each other. She told him that she noticed a strong resemblance between Miller and her hero, Abraham Lincoln—a touching tribute to the playwright, who suggested several books for her to read about the sixteenth president of the United States.

Marilyn told Natasha after the party, "He held my toe and we just looked into each other's eyes." Natasha did not have to remind Marilyn that Arthur was married and lived in New York. Even so, they corresponded and spoke on the telephone occasionally. She admired men like Miller—the serious intellectual type who seemed to enjoy talking to her about any number of topics other than making movies.

Marilyn was very conscious of her shady reputation that reflected her roles on the screen. She was a dumb blonde and an easy lay. She was Joe Schenck's "mistress" and she used Johnny Hyde. If Hollywood insiders knew the *whole* truth, Marilyn might have been stoned to death on the corner of Hollywood and Vine. Spyros Skouras was seen going in and out of her new residence at the Beverly Carlton. Skouras had, more or less, taken Schenck's place.

Marilyn was also seen in the company of Howard Hughes, who furthered her career "behind the scenes." There was much speculation that the mysterious Hughes convinced Natasha to leave her job at Columbia and paid her to coach Marilyn.

Hughes could be an affable fellow. He sent flowers to Marilyn, flew her and Natasha off to a Palm Springs mansion staffed with servants. His meetings alone with Marilyn were the cloak-and-dagger type—whisked off in an old car to a secluded airport where Howard was waiting in the cockpit, destination unknown. Marilyn returned from one of these mysterious trips with a chapped face that she blamed on Howard's five-o'clock shadow.

Hughes often carried a case of jewelry for his women, giving them a choice of diamonds, gold and rubies. It's not known if Marilyn was given this privilege, but Hughes gave her a pin. Though she was not materialistic, it aroused her curiosity and she had the pin appraised. It was worth only $500—a paltry value considering Howard's generosity with the women he wanted. Most likely Marilyn gave in too easily, because Gene Tierney, Ava Gardner and Lana Turner found Hughes to be the sultan of Hollywood.

Hughes was obsessed with big breasts, but he was not intimate with his two busty movie discoveries, Jean Harlow and Jane Russell. He liked recently divorced women, "wet decks," as he referred to them. Howard ran after Ava Gardner when she left Mickey Rooney, Lana Turner after her divorce from Artie Shaw, and Susan Hayward following her parting from husband Jess Barker. Though he was considered a cocksman, Hughes was afraid if he put too much effort into lovemaking, it might exhaust him. With most of his girlfriends, Marilyn included, it was hit and run, but if Hughes concentrated on one woman for any length of time, he was a magnificent lover.

Howard's close friend Brian Evans (not his real name) is a Canadian tycoon and was a backer of Broadway plays in the fifties. He dated Grace Kelly (and this author), who found in him a trusted friend.

"I know Howard had bodyguards watching Monroe's house for a brief time," Brian said. "He was amused that actor Peter Lawford was turned away. Hughes didn't have much to say about Marilyn other than she wasn't as busty as she appeared, but he thought she had potential in films. Howard didn't pursue Monroe because she wasn't his type. He preferred the indifference and hot temperament of gals like Ava Gardner, whom he had followed day and night. If he gave her a bad time, she gave it right back to him and went on her merry way.

Howard said that Monroe not only wanted but needed his undivided attention and that was something he was unable to give anyone."

Brian said Hughes had spies in the powder rooms of every nightclub in Hollywood, where shoptalk and gossip reigned supreme. "But Howard was interested in business matters such as what studios were losing money, the stars' salaries and contracts and personal affairs. All the movie moguls were underhanded, but Howard was involved in other business ventures besides RKO so he had to go to extremes."

Marilyn wanted to please Hughes. He wielded more power than most Hollywood moguls because he was a multimillionaire in his own right.

How much he had to do with getting Marilyn a good part in *Clash by Night* at RKO isn't certain, but it surely is not coincidental, either. Columnist Sidney Skolsky, a very close friend of Marilyn's, claims most of the credit. He arranged a meeting with RKO's production assistant Jerry Wald who thought Marilyn could play the girlfriend of Barbara Stanwyck's kid brother, Keith Andes.

Clash by Night was the screen adaptation of a play by Clifford Odets. To lift the film's burdensome theme of middle-age poverty and adultery, Jerry Wald suggested adding Peggy's character. He hoped to attract young moviegoers who might be less than enthusiastic over the trials and tribulations of Barbara Stanwyck's boring marriage to fisherman Paul Douglas and her affair with movie projectionist Robert Ryan.

After her encounter with Bette Davis, Marilyn was terrified to work in a film with another tough cookie—Barbara Stanwyck. Both actresses were reputed to be no-nonsense perfectionists. Marilyn was warned that Stanwyck had recently filed for divorce from Robert Taylor and was going through a very difficult period. But Natasha assured Marilyn that she would be with her on the set at all times and not to worry.

Stanwyck was not a problem. It was Monroe who tripped

herself up repeatedly and forgot her lines even with the help of cue cards. "She was awkward," Stanwyck said in an interview. "She couldn't get out of her own way. She wasn't disciplined, and she was often late. She drove Bob Ryan, Paul Douglas and myself out of our minds ... but she didn't do it viciously, and there was sort of a magic about her which we all recognized at once. Her phobias, or whatever they were, came later; she seemed just a carefree kid, and she owned the world."

Director Fritz Lang (*Fury, You Only Live Twice, Western Union* and *The Woman in the Window,* among others) rehearsed the cast every evening for the following day, but Marilyn faced the camera with a different approach. Lang reserved his temper until he noticed Natasha hidden behind the camera giving signals to Marilyn. Lang ordered Natasha off the set and told her not to come back. Marilyn asked him sweetly if it was all right to consult her acting coach. Lang replied, "Absolutely not! When we're finished rehearsing for tomorrow I don't want that woman twisting things around." Marilyn stood there in a daze until Lang said, "Either she [Natasha] goes or I go."

Without Natasha to guide and protect her, Marilyn was beside herself with fear. Lang, a victim of Nazi Germany, was a director of realistic drama bordering on violence, a master of *film noir*. An actress of Stanwyck's magnitude was eager to work with Lang, who she considered a genius. But for a newcomer with nothing other than her physical attributes, it would have been sheer hell. Lang, however, wanted Marilyn from the start; some sources claim it was his idea to cast her in the role of Peggy. He had more compassion for Stanwyck, who had to put up with Marilyn's tardiness and many retakes.

Adding to the tension was Paul Douglas, who disliked Marilyn intensely. "Who is she to get star billing?" he complained. Fortunately, he had no scenes with her, but Douglas flashed dirty looks in her direction. It was Stanwyck who managed to keep him from exploding. Robert Ryan liked Marilyn, saying, "She's somethin' else!"

During production of *Clash by Night*, rumors about an actress posing nude for a calendar spread around Hollywood like wildfire. Reporters saw the pictures and did not wait for an official identification. It was Marilyn Monroe, and they descended on the movie set. The calendar wasn't mentioned, but Marilyn knew that someone was planning to reveal the truth about her fifty-dollar indiscretion. Not only did this add to her tension, but the embarrassment of having the press swarming over her while ignoring Stanwyck. Robert Ryan said, "The calendar business was no secret in Hollywood, but the public didn't know about it. One of the reporters asked me, 'Where's the babe with the big tits?' He didn't even know her name."

While the brass at Fox decided how to handle the impending scandal, Marilyn played a beauty-contest winner in *We're Not Married*, with David Wayne. She got second billing to Richard Widmark in *Don't Bother to Knock*, the story of a deranged baby-sitter. Marilyn was not prepared for this demanding role and it would never suit her. But what happened during production put Marilyn on a pedestal with the memory of the late Jean Harlow, who rubbed her nipples with ice cubes to make them hard before going on the movie set.

Jerry Wald at RKO got an anonymous phone call from a man who said he would expose the nude woman on calendars gracing bars all over the country if he did not receive $10,000. Why the call to Wald at RKO? Because his film *Clash by Night* was about to be released. There was a strong possibility the movie would be boycotted or banned. RKO did not have as much to lose as Fox, who had Marilyn signed to a seven-year contract. The morals clause was reason enough to drop her, but the studio had time and money invested in two unreleased Monroe films, *We're Not Married* and *Don't Bother to Knock*.

There was talk of not releasing *Clash by Night* and canceling Marilyn's contract. As usual, there are many versions of what happened and who came up with a plausible solution. But there is no doubt that Marilyn pulled it off. Who devised and

arranged her interview with Aline Mosby of United Press is up
for grabs, but Jerry Wald said it was Mosby who wanted to print
the story. He suggested she call Fox for a personal interview
with Monroe, who was advised by the front office to deny
everything. Marilyn wanted to tell the truth and, surprisingly,
Zanuck agreed with her.

Marilyn did not want her meeting with Mosby to appear
prepared or formal. The women chatted for a few minutes
before Marilyn asked Mosby to go to the powder room with her.
Behind the door marked LADIES, Marilyn confided that she
posed in the nude for money to make a payment on her car.

On March 13, 1952, Aline Mosby printed Marilyn Monroe's
confession in a straightforward article. That the young model
needed money to eat, pay her rent and recover her repossessed
car was not enough to capture public sympathy, but Marilyn's
statement—"I was told I should deny I posed … but I'd rather
be honest about it"—tipped the scales in her favor. Maybe she
made a mistake posing in the nude, but she defied her advisors
and was honest about it.

Two months later another revelation about Marilyn surfaced.
She had been publicized as an orphan who never knew her
mother and father. "From a reliable source," Zanuck said to
her, "I've been informed that your mother is living in a mental
institution. Is it true?"

Marilyn nodded.

"If there's anything else I should know, I'd like to hear it
from you now."

The story broke in May of 1952, and once again Marilyn
issued a statement that made you wish she *were* an orphan. "I
didn't know my mother. She spent years as an invalid in a state
hospital. I was raised in a series of foster homes."

And so moviegoers lined up at the box office to see the sexy
nude calendar girl whose mother was locked up in a nut house.
Clash by Night received sour reviews by critics who compared
Odets' play to the movie, but the *New York Post* review read,

"... that gorgeous example of bathing beauty art (in denim), Marilyn Monroe, is a real acting threat to the season's screen blondes." And the *New York Daily News* reported, "Marilyn Monroe, who is the new blonde bombshell of Hollywood, manages to look alluring in blue jeans. She plays Peggy with assurance."

It is interesting to note that critics labeled Marilyn "bathing beauty" and "blonde bombshell" even though she wore shirts and jeans, and despite the fact her movie roles to date were not sexy. It appears the critics were judging the celebrated calendar rather than her performance as Peggy in *Clash by Night*.

Marilyn's career would not have survived without the support of Howard Hughes and Fox moguls. It was Hughes who stood by Robert Mitchum in 1948 when the actor was jailed for possession of marijuana. Instead of invoking the "morals clause" in Bob's RKO contract, Hughes released his latest movie *Rachel and the Stranger*, which went over so big, it was held over in major cities. Concerned about Mitchum's health, Hughes paid a secret visit to him in jail and loaned Bob money to buy a house for his family.

The "morals clause" has often been mentioned in books pertaining to Hollywood celebrities, but seldom defined. Depending on the studio, the wording might vary, but this clause is quite explicit.

The artist agrees to conduct himself with due regard to public conventions and morals and agrees that he will not commit any act or thing that will degrade him in society, or bring him into public hatred, contempt, scorn or ridicule, that will tend to shock, insult or offend the community or ridicule public morals or decency, or prejudice the producer (studio's name) or the motion picture industry in general.

There were occasions when the American public took matters into their own hands as they did when Ingrid Bergman deserted her husband and daughter to be with her lover in Europe. Ingrid gave birth to Roberto Rossellini's son in Italy, and the American public was outraged. They did not welcome Bergman back to the United States for six years.

The nude calendar, however, made Marilyn every man's desire, and her homeless childhood provoked sympathy from women who might otherwise have boycotted her films.

But this was no surprise to Howard Hughes.

7

Who's on First?

In the midst of the worldwide publicity about Marilyn, she checked into the Cedars of Lebanon Hospital for an appendectomy. The nurses knew she had posed for a nude calendar and couldn't wait to find out if their patient was "blonde all over."

In the operating room, the nurse in attendance was about to find out. Turning down the sheet she was shocked to see a piece of paper taped to Marilyn's stomach. The note, addressed to the doctor, was a pathetic plea to cut as little as possible. Marilyn begged him to avoid large scars and thanked him with all her heart.

The note represents an obsession Marilyn had for her body that she described as her "magic friend." Sex did not enter into it from her point of view. It was the attention and compliments she received from strange men in bars. Then it was the admiration from photographers and later the astonishing reaction from powerful men who were accustomed to beautiful women, but ogled *her*. And now it was the nude calendar that made her body a work of art. She had posed for this picture when she was three years younger. Marilyn became more aware than ever before that she had to preserve her most valuable asset—her body.

The operation in April of 1952 was a success, the scar was barely visible, but the attending nurse found out that the blonde bombshell was *not* blonde all over. From then on Marilyn bleached her pubic hair.

A few days later the surgeon who operated on her had good news. "You can go home in a few days, Marilyn."

"I can't leave," she said.

"Why not?" he asked.

"Because I can't pay my bill."

"Why don't you ask the studio to take care of it?"

"Do you think I should?" She blinked.

"Why not? You're very important to them."

Marilyn wasn't so sure, but she placed a call to someone at Fox. The bill was paid and a limousine was waiting to take her home.

In the note to her doctor preceding the operation, Marilyn mentioned her ovaries because there were possible complications in the pelvic area, and a gynecologist was standing by during the appendectomy.

Precisely when Marilyn had a tubal ligation to prevent pregnancy isn't known. By her own admission it was Johnny Hyde who advised the operation. Many Monroe historians theorize she had it done at the same time as the appendectomy. Others think Hyde arranged and paid for everything including her cosmetic surgery before he died. (Marilyn eventually had surgery to reverse the tubal ligation, a complicated procedure in the fifties.)

Marilyn's next film was the comical *Monkey Business* about a chemist (Cary Grant) who accidentally discovers a formula for youth. He drinks the brew and goes on a merry spree with Marilyn to the dismay of his wife (Ginger Rogers), who drinks the magic concoction to keep up with them.

Marilyn is bosomy and young, of course. Her role as Charles Coburn's secretary is summed up when he hands her a letter and says, "Find someone to type this."

Marilyn is a natural in *Monkey Business*. She oozes sex, but is sweet and shy. Her character doesn't know about the youth brew, and she glides through the often silly rumpus with a wide-eyed look of innocence and gaiety.

Cary Grant, in an interview with Earl Wilson, did not comment on movie marquees ignoring him, and featuring instead MARILYN MONROE IN MONKEY BUSINESS. Besides, Wilson was more interested in how Cary felt about the nude calendar controversy. "There are lots of models who pose in the art studios for hours," Grant said. "Nobody thinks wrong of that!"

"So, you've come out for nude calendars?" Wilson heckled.

"What the hell is wrong with looking at a beautiful body if it really is beautiful? I found Marilyn a very shy and rather smart girl," Grant said. "A real person. A very dear person. She reads every book that comes out. The publicity about her is far in excess of her talents, but not in excess of her sexual impact. They're all telling her to wear something revealing and the child wants to be in blue jeans and an old flannel shirt. It's nice to know," Grant said, "that I'm happily married." (Grant was then married to his third wife, actress Betsy Drake. They separated in 1958 and divorced three years later.)

Grant said there was talk about a movie, entitled *Mother Knows Best*, with Jane Russell and Marilyn Monroe as the daughters, and Mae West as the mother. Everybody thought it was a sensational idea. "I don't play mothers," Miss West warbled.

Grant told Earl Wilson, "I hope Marilyn will save her money and her sex appeal like Mae West did. She must never play mothers, either, until she's a great-grandmother."

An unknown Hugh Hefner paid $500 for Marilyn's "art calendar" that appeared in the first issue of *Playboy*. She agreed to sign the cover picture of her posing fully clothed, but would not admit she had autographed the calendar for friends.

Marilyn told the press she was worried and nervous, "… but I did nothing wrong."

Joe DiMaggio retired from baseball in 1951 at the age of thirty-six. When he met Marilyn a year later, Joe had been divorced for almost a decade. A hero in his own right, he had never had a problem getting dates with beautiful women, but Joe was no different from any other red-blooded American male. He wanted to meet Marilyn Monroe, too. The opportunity arose through a mutual friend, agent David March, who arranged a blind date for dinner at Villa Nova, an Italian restaurant in Los Angeles.

Marilyn was not enthusiastic. She'd heard of DiMaggio but wasn't sure if he played baseball or football and she cared less. "I don't like the way athletes dress," she told March. "They have big muscles and wear loud clothes." But Marilyn agreed anyway. When she failed to show up, March called her. Marilyn complained about being tired after working all day at the studio. But she showed up two hours later looking radiantly beautiful. Joe was impressed, but maintained his cool. It was Marilyn who was delightfully surprised to meet a distinguished gentleman with salt-and-pepper hair and wearing a subdued business suit. Yankee great Mickey Mantle said that Joe dressed like a senator.

Joseph Paul DiMaggio was the eighth of nine children born to Sicilian immigrants in Martinez, California, on November 25, 1914. His father, a fisherman, moved the family to nearby San Francisco when Joe was a year old. The elder DiMaggio expected his son to become a fisherman, but Joe was uneasy on boats. Legend has it that he spent hours alone on the beach with a baseball using a broken oar for a bat. He was not coached and he didn't practice. A childhood pal said, "Joe played ball, simple as that."

At the age of nineteen, DiMaggio was playing with the San

Francisco Seals and got on base in sixty-one consecutive games, breaking the Pacific Coast record. Three years later (1936) the New York Yankees "bought" Joe D. for $25,000. In 1941, he broke another record by hitting safely in fifty-six consecutive games.

Other than DiMaggio's athletic achievements and his involvement with Marilyn Monroe, little has been written about his personal life.

Joe married twenty-one-year-old blonde starlet Dorothy Arnold on November 19, 1939, after a two-year courtship. She told the press, "I have every intention of pursuing my career," and then added, "Joe does, too." Reporters had all they could do to control themselves. Was it possible the greatest ball player in the world was staying in the game? What the press saw that day was a pretty blonde girl who could sing, dance and act a little bit. Her only claim to fame was being Mrs. Joe DiMaggio, but in all fairness to Dorothy, she wanted him as much as, if not more than, a film career.

The marriage was rocky from the beginning. When Joe wasn't on the road with the Yankees, he wanted to live in San Francisco. Dorothy preferred Los Angeles. They settled in New York City where Joe spent most of his spare time at Toots Shor with the boys. Dorothy hoped the birth of Joseph Paul DiMaggio, Jr., on October 23, 1941, would salvage the marriage and give her husband a reason for coming home, but Joe did not change his life-style.

Dorothy made several trips to Reno with every intention of getting a divorce. Joe always talked her out of it and she came back to him. While his marriage was hanging by a thread, the Japanese bombed Pearl Harbor. Joe, classified 3-A, would be drafted after all the single men were inducted. Waiting to receive his "Greetings" letter took its toll on DiMaggio. His comment to friends about "getting it over with and enlisting" leaked to the press. Joe denied ever saying he would volunteer "but I'm going to try to get into the service somehow."

DiMaggio wasn't making much sense because he was trying once again to get his wife back. Dorothy had taken Joe, Jr., and set up residence in Reno.

Nineteen forty-two was not a good year for DiMaggio. The Yankees lost the World Series to the St. Louis Cardinals, and Joe was suffering from the first stage of ulcers. Swallowing his pride, he faced Dorothy in Reno and begged her not to go through with the divorce because she meant the world to him.

In January of 1943, the DiMaggios reconciled. A month later Joe reported for army duty and was stationed at the Santa Ana Army Airfield in Southern California. Dorothy settled in nearby Los Angeles, but rarely did Joe make an effort to see her.

After his promotion to staff sergeant, DiMaggio was transferred to Hawaii, where he played baseball for the Seventh Air Force Team. While World War II raged, Joe had only to fight with the umpires, but a war of his own ravaged his gut. When his wife filed for divorce in October of 1943, DiMaggio did not contest the action, but he was hospitalized with bleeding ulcers. He longed for Dorothy almost as much as he ached to be in Yankee uniform again. After his discharge from the service two years later, he managed both.

Joe courted Dorothy, who cherished his attention, but most likely he did not propose again. Her second and third marriages ended in divorce and, through it all, Joe was still in love with Dorothy. They were considering a "permanent reconciliation" in 1951 when he retired from baseball.

But, of course, Joe's blind date with Marilyn Monroe changed everything. She had her car that night and offered to give him a lift. They drove around for hours and talked, ending up making love in the backseat. DiMaggio was not known to brag about his sexual conquests (and he had his fair share), but he told his cronies that he was intimate with Marilyn on their first date. This might have been expected, but Joe broke a precedent by calling her the following morning.

When Marilyn was asked what they did after leaving the

restaurant she replied, "Well, we didn't discuss baseball."

She and Joe saw each other every night until he returned to New York on business. He sent flowers and called her every day. The romance was a press agent's dream. The publicity staff at 20th Century-Fox worked overtime getting the couple's pictures in the newspapers, and writing feature articles about Marilyn Monroe, our American Cinderella, and her Prince Charming, Yankee All-Star Joe DiMaggio. He proposed marriage on their first date, but she wasn't ready for the glass slipper just yet.

Marilyn, who literally skyrocketed to fame within a few short months, was trying to get her bearings. She left the Beverly Carlton and moved to an apartment in the Hollywood Hills with actress Shelley Winters, whose recent affair with Burt Lancaster had ended when she found out his wife was pregnant. Winters evened the score by having a fling with Marlon Brando.

Shelley and Marilyn had long talks about their heartbreaking love affairs, and how they usually got emotionally involved. Shelley commented, "There is no earthly reason why we shouldn't just concentrate on our careers and sleep with whoever is attractive to us, like men do." They decided to each make a list of men they would like to bed down.

Marilyn chose Zero Mostel, Eli Wallach, Charles Boyer, Jean Renoir, Lee Strasberg, Nick Ray, John Huston, Elia Kazan, Harry Belafonte, Yves Montand, Charles Bickford, Ernest Hemingway, Charles Laughton, Clifford Odets, Dean Jagger, Arthur Miller and Albert Einstein.

Shelley read the list and exclaimed, "There's no way you can sleep with Albert Einstein. He's the most famous scientist of the century, and besides he's an old man."

"That has nothing to do with it," Marilyn said. "I hear he's very healthy!"

Marilyn did have a brief affair in 1951 with Elia Kazan, who directed Arthur Miller's first stage play *All My Sons* in 1947, and then organized the famous Actors Studio with Lee

Strasberg in New York. Kazan also directed such acclaimed films as *A Tree Grows in Brooklyn, Gentleman's Agreement, A Streetcar Named Desire, East of Eden* and *On the Waterfront.*

When Marilyn was seeing Kazan, he was forty-two, married and the father of four children. She was attracted to his genius as a director and his resemblance to Johnny Hyde. Kazan was a ladies' man, but he was especially fond of Marilyn. He appreciated her sense of humor, natural wit and her ability to listen. She was always making notes, an admirable trait, but one that would get her into trouble one day.

Marilyn's involvment with Kazan was not serious. They were rarely seen together in public and she told very few people about the affair. (This meant everyone in Hollywood knew about it.) They remained friends throughout the years and she later joined the Actors Studio in New York on his recommendation.

Nineteen fifty-two was the turning point for Marilyn in all aspects. Fred Karger, whom she still loved, married actress Jane Wyman, who had divorced Ronald Reagan in 1948.

Coincidentally, Marilyn was leaving Chasen's restaurant with columnist Sidney Skolsky when she found out the loud music was coming from Karger's wedding reception. She crashed the event to congratulate and kiss the groom. Skolsky said this was not typical of Marilyn, who was still paying off the watch she'd given Karger.

But the public did not get a glimpse of a rejected Marilyn. On the contrary. The daily press fed their readers news for which they hungered—Joe DiMaggio's courtship of Marilyn Monroe, but he avoided being seen in public with her. His feelings were compounded when Dorothy saw a picture in the newspaper of Joe, Jr., with his father and Marilyn sitting poolside. Dorothy tried to prevent DiMaggio from seeing his son, claiming in court that the boy had been exposed to persons with immoral reputations (i.e., Marilyn). The judge ruled against her and commented that she never should have divorced DiMaggio in the first place.

Joe bombarded Marilyn with flowers and phone calls, but she took his attention in stride and often his roses were left to wilt in the florist's delivery box.

The Yankee hero was a clean-cut modest fellow to fans around the world, and Marilyn soon got a taste of Joe's winning determination. She suspected he was checking up on her, asking too many questions about where she was and with whom. What Marilyn needed these days was an escort, but DiMaggio was not interested in the "job."

Though Marilyn liked her men to dress with distinction, she wore low-cut dresses that clung to her derrière. DiMaggio wanted no part of this sex circus. He detested Hollywood premieres and parties. In or out of love, Joe refused to compromise. He and Marilyn spent quiet evenings together away from the crowds. She went along with this arrangement because Joe was a devoted guy and a satisfying lover.

Marilyn was too busy with her career to give serious consideration to Joe's marriage proposals. She filmed *O. Henry's Full House*, featuring four tales with surprise endings—O. Henry's forte. Charles Laughton plays a well-dressed bum who tries to get himself arrested so he can spend the cold winter months in jail. One of his unsuccessful attempts is accosting a stunning streetwalker portrayed by Marilyn.

O. Henry's Full House was a fine film with a star-studded cast—Dale Robertson, David Wayne, Richard Widmark, Anne Baxter, Jean Peters, Farley Granger, Jeanne Crain, Laughton and Monroe. The *New York Times* wrote, "These stories need no introduction. They stand on their own." Marilyn did, too. Seeing her in this film today is a rare treat.

When Shelley Winters decided to marry Italian actor Vittorio Gassman, Marilyn moved to a pool suite in the elegant Bel Air Hotel. She could well afford the $750 a month while she looked for an apartment.

Marilyn was having affairs with numerous men at this time.

Greek actor Nico Minardos told author Anthony Summers that Marilyn was a "lousy lay," but a beautiful, bright and shrewd girl. Nico said that Marilyn wanted to get married, but he thought she was mixed-up and, besides, "I was never going to let myself become 'Mr. Monroe.' "

Another visitor to her hotel suite was Spyros Skouras. Marilyn tried her best to seduce Darryl Zanuck, who forced himself to be pleasant now that she was a valuable asset to Fox, but he ignored her. "I would have done anything," she told a friend, "… anything he wanted. I tried, but he wasn't interested. He was the only guy who wasn't and I never knew why."

Zanuck put Marilyn in dumb-blonde roles because that's what he thought she was. Maybe his reasoning was wrong, but his concept of Monroe's image on the screen was accurate. If she had seduced Zanuck, it's doubtful he would have changed his mind. "Nobody discovered Monroe," he said. "She earned her own way to stardom."

Marilyn did, however, convince Zanuck to put Natasha Lytess on Fox's payroll. She relied on her coach and would not do a film without Natasha. There was a bond between the women that has been partially misinterpreted. Marilyn told her maid Lena Pepitone that she had given in to Natasha's advances, knowing it was wrong. "She got really jealous about the men I saw," Marilyn said. "She thought she was my husband. She was a great teacher, but that part of it ruined it for us. I got scared of her, had to get away."

Pepitone defended Marilyn. "Any warmth shown to her, by any person, regardless of his or her sex, was welcomed and cherished. Marilyn needed to be loved by anyone who was sincere."

Someone who filled this need was Robert Slatzer, a young reporter from Ohio.

8

Bob

It was the summer of 1946 when a nineteen-year-old junior at Ohio State University was hustling work in Los Angeles. "I was trying to make some extra money by writing newspaper articles about Hollywood celebrities," Slatzer said. "I had an appointment at 20th Century-Fox and was sitting in the lobby when a pretty young girl with light brown hair rushed through the front door and stumbled. The contents of her old scrapbook went flying in all directions. I helped gather up her clippings and photos, and we sat together in the waiting room. She introduced herself as Norma Jeane Mortenson."

Apparently Bob's midwestern earthiness appealed to her because she accepted a date with him that night. They dined at a restaurant in Malibu and drove along the ocean.

"Let's park the car and go for a swim," she chirped.

"But I didn't bring a bathing suit," Bob said innocently.

She laughed and they strolled on the beach until suddenly Marilyn took off her clothes and went into the water. "C'mon!" she called to Bob, who stripped down to his shorts. Today he admits, "I was embarrassed and yet we made love on the beach later. It just happened. Nothing was deliberate or planned. There was a mutual attraction and trust between us from the very start. We dated frequently during the next several weeks.

Every time I took her home and asked when we'd see each other again, Marilyn gave me a peculiar answer: 'Maybe I'll get back to you sometime.' What I didn't know was that she was living with her adopted aunt, Ana Lower, who was very, very strict and disgusted by the late hours her 'niece' was keeping."

Late one night Bob heard a knock on his door at the Hollywood Plaza Hotel and there stood a forlorn Norma Jeane Mortenson with her suitcase. "Aunt Ana threw me out and I have nowhere else to go," she said.

Slatzer felt partially responsible for what happened and wanted to help her, but he had a job with Brush-Moore newspapers in Ohio and wanted to finish college. "We talked about marriage," he said, "but money was the big drawback. Frankly, I wasn't certain what line of work I wanted to pursue and was in no position to support a wife. Marilyn was set on modeling and getting into films. So, I went home after my newspaper assignment, but returned to Hollywood for Christmas."

Robert Slatzer was born in Marion, Ohio, on April 4, 1928, a blood relation (on his mother's side) to President Warren G. Harding. The elder Slatzer, a building contractor, hoped one of his two sons would take an interest in the family business, but Bob became a cub reporter for the Marion *Star*, writing everything from obituaries to weather forecasts. His brother was an accountant.

In 1943, the Marion *Star* assigned sixteen-year-old Slatzer to cover the filming of *Home in Indiana* at the Marion County Fair Grounds. June Haver made her debut in this colorful 20th Century-Fox classic with Jeanne Crain, Lon McCallister and Walter Brennan. Director Henry Hathaway (*Wing and a Prayer, Kiss of Death, Call Northside 777, Niagara, True Grit* and *How the West Was Won*, among others) befriended Bob, who confided his frustrations to Hathaway: "I want to join the service, but my parents won't give their consent. There's a war going on and I wish like hell I was eighteen." Hathaway helped him get a job in Fox's mail room in the summer of 1944. This was Slatzer's introduction to Hollywood.

Classmate Jean Peters (Miss Ohio State of 1945) suggested Bob focus on photo-journalism, a combination reporter and a photographer, affording him better jobs and wages. Jean signed a Fox contract in 1946 and made her smashing debut with Tyrone Power in *Captain of Castile*, but kept in touch with Slatzer.

When the war was over, Bob decided to spend his summers in Los Angeles. Brush-Moore newspapers wanted him to do a series of celebrity interviews in Hollywood. He was on this assignment in 1946 when Norma Jeane Mortenson stumbled into his life.

Pretty girls with good figures were plentiful in Hollywood, and Norma Jeane Mortenson was just another one who would most likely fail. Slatzer did not fall in love with a myth or a movie goddess. Like Jim Dougherty before him, Bob was attracted to a delightful young lady whose zest for living and recognition did not camouflage her vulnerability. Marilyn would never lose this neediness and childlike quality.

Of every legendary movie actress, someone has said, "... there was something that set her apart from the others," but Norma Jeane Mortenson had yet to reach that stature. Nonetheless Slatzer took odd jobs to help her out financially. "I stuck to my writing," he said, "but I also unloaded bananas and picked cotton, worked as a waiter and was a 'roughneck' in the oil fields. I gave Marilyn what I could to pay for her acting lessons. She lived with me or I lived with her, depending on which one of us was working."

Then Marilyn met Fred Karger and she moved in with his family. This interlude gave Slatzer a chance to concentrate on his own career. After selling his first screenplay to Monogram Studios in 1948, Bob was able to afford a nice home in the Hollywood Hills and began mixing with an intellectual crowd of writers, directors and producers. Marilyn was a frequent guest, but she felt inferior to Bob's friends. "She was anxious to learn," he said, "but no one had taken the time to teach her. She wanted to borrow some of my books and we discussed them in depth. One of our favorites was *The Rubáiyát* by Omar Khayyám on the grounds that while books could not teach us to enjoy life, they could at least help us endure it."

A close buddy of Slatzer's said that Marilyn and Bob now moved in different circles: "He was a director, writer and producer. He was making a damn good living, but suddenly he packed up and went back to Ohio."

Slatzer explains, "I was seeing Marilyn, but after the nude calendar exposure, she was being used by the studio, the press and the public. Marilyn was on a merry-go-round and to avoid getting on it with her, I went back to Ohio. We talked regularly on the phone at nights because we were both insomniacs. She was a big star now but she still sought my advice on many things, including what good books to read."

Slatzer had no problem getting dates with other women. Of German-Dutch descent, he was a tall husky fellow with dark brown hair and eyes, a "man's man" who often went on fishing trips with Gary Cooper, Robert Taylor and Clark Gable, all of whom were skilled with a reel and rifle.

Bob is reluctant to discuss his relationship with Jean Peters (the future Mrs. Howard Hughes), but their friendship endures to this day. She called him from Hollywood, in June of 1952, with an invitation. "I'm making a movie in Niagara Falls," Jean said. "Henry [Hathaway] is directing so we'll have a big ol' family reunion."

Slatzer decided to make the trip before Marilyn got in touch with him about her starring role opposite Jean in *Niagara*. "I'll get you a room at the General Brock Hotel where I'm staying," she said, "and I'll pick you up at the airport." Possibly Marilyn heard about Bob and Jean Peters, although this relationship was platonic, according to him. But there is no doubt that Marilyn needed Slatzer, whose even temperament was a leveler for her fluctuating moods. Who else had helped her through the bad times and asked nothing in return?

On her way to Niagara Falls, Marilyn stopped off in New York to see DiMaggio. He was disillusioned over her playing a prostitute in *O. Henry's Full House* and disgusted with her role as an unfaithful wife in *Niagara*. Wearing cheap tight dresses and singing to an absent lover while her husband (Joseph Cotten) suffers in silence, Marilyn established her sensuous image. For a few famous seconds and 150 feet of cobblestone, she slithers away from the camera with that familiar wobbly walk, enticing any man who was still breathing—every man except DiMaggio, who was sickened by the very thought of it.

Marilyn told Bob about her stopover in New York. "I may be selfish," she said, "because I'd rather have Joe as a good friend. But he wants things his way. If I did marry him, I think he'll lock me up in a room."

"What did you do in New York?" Bob asked casually.

"Joe enjoys hanging around with his old baseball buddies at Toots Shor. That trip to New York really wore me out."

"I promised to meet Jean Peters for a late dinner. Would you like to come along?"

"Too tired." Marilyn yawned. "I like working with Jean. She's great."

Bob was on the set every day. Unfortunately, Natasha Lytess was on hand, also. Henry Hathaway did not want "that goddamned Russian woman" around when they were working. Marilyn still relied on Natasha, but Hathaway did not allow sentiment to change his mind about barring Lytess from the set. "To be a good director," he said, "you've got to be a bastard. I'm a bastard and I know it."

Before leaving Hollywood, Hathaway spoke to Marilyn about her wardrobe in *Niagara*, which was her first technicolor film. "I want you to wear your own clothes," he said.

"I don't have any clothes," Marilyn exclaimed. He didn't

believe her so she took him home. All she had were slacks and sweaters. In the back of the closet was a black suit. "I bought that for Johnny's funeral," she said. (Marilyn wore this suit at the end of *Niagara* when she is murdered by Joseph Cotten.) Marilyn told Hathaway, "I borrow clothes from the studio if I have to go someplace special." And so the director bought her a simple wardrobe that included the unforgettable red satin low-cut clinging dress. In the movie Jean Peters describes it as "the kind you have to start making plans to wear when you're thirteen years old."

Marilyn and Bob did a fair amount of drinking in her suite at the General Brock Hotel. Without any warning, she said, "We should get married and spend our honeymoon right here in Niagara Falls." Bob assumed it was the booze talking and did not pursue the subject.

In July, the cast and crew of *Niagara* returned to the Fox studios in Hollywood to shoot interior scenes. Slatzer reported four days late for work at the Columbia Dispatch and was given his walking papers. Marilyn considered this an omen and begged Bob to resume his career in Hollywood.

Meanwhile, gossip columnists continued to link Monroe and DiMaggio, who was pursuing her relentlessly. Slatzer said she got her dates mixed up one night and he came face-to-face with Joe on her doorstep. She let them both in, and while Bob made himself a drink, Joe tore into Marilyn. "How does he know where the bar is?" They argued until Marilyn told both men to go home. Bob didn't want any trouble, either, but outside Joe glared at him. "He's a big guy." Slatzer laughed. "And I wasn't taking any chances so I said, 'Good night, slugger.' He drove off in a huff." Later that night Marilyn called Bob to apologize. She said that Joe went into a rage if she looked at another man, and that his possessiveness would make a permanent relationship impossible. Joe returned to New York in September to get ready for his radio commentary on the World Series between the Yankees and the Dodgers.

On Friday, October 3, Marilyn and Bob stayed up all night drinking. "I'm tired of sleeping around," she exclaimed. "Why don't we get married?" He realized Marilyn was serious when they discussed when and where. Yuma, Arizona, was popular with eloping celebrities, but Marilyn was leary of the publicity, so they settled for Mexico. After breakfast and gallons of coffee, they had sobered up. Marilyn looked at Bob and asked, "Should we?" He didn't know whether she meant "Should we get married?" or "Should we hit the road?" Bob knew it was reality when she handed him her suitcase and walked out to his car. Slatzer said, "Marilyn wasn't wearing any makeup, her hair was pulled straight back in a ponytail and she was dressed simply in a white blouse under a beige sweater and black slacks. It was like turning the clock back six years and I was eloping with Norma Jeane Mortenson."

They drove to Tijuana in Bob's 1948 maroon Packard convertible with the top down. Along the way, Marilyn turned on the radio and Joe D.'s voice came over loud and clear. "I can't get rid of him!" She laughed.

"That's the World Series," Bob yelped. "Leave it on."

They listened to the ball game as they drove south of the border. After checking into The Foreign Club Hotel, they took a swim and had a few drinks. Then they walked around Tijuana until Bob spotted a sign, ATTORNEY—MARRIAGES AND DIVORCES. The office walls were a drab green and the floors were bare. The seedy-looking lawyer said they needed two witnesses and if there was a problem his wife was available for five dollars.

"I bought two gold wedding bands for fifteen dollars a-piece," Slatzer said. "We walked around for a while and that's when we bumped into an old friend, Noble 'Kid' Chissell, who was in town looking up an old Navy buddy. He agreed to be a witness and we headed back to the law office. Along the way Marilyn went into a Catholic church to pray. She signed her name 'Norma Jeane Mortenson' on the papers written in

Spanish, and then we went through the unimpressive three-minute ceremony. Someone had stolen Marilyn's shoes that she'd left outside the church door, so she was married in her bare feet."

That night the newlyweds checked out of The Foreign Club Hotel, drove down the serene Pacific Coast and registered as man and wife at The Rosarita Beach Hotel. They agreed that their marriage should be kept a secret for the time being. They were both leasing houses and could get away with it—or so they thought.

On Tuesday, Marilyn reported for wardrobe fittings on *Gentlemen Prefer Blondes* at Fox. If she had confided only in her loyal friend and makeup man Whitey Snyder about the elopement, her secret might have been safe. But Marilyn told a few other people whom she trusted, and the news soon reached Darryl Zanuck, who demanded to see her immediately. Marilyn called Bob in tears, and he rushed to Fox.

Slatzer was no stranger to Zanuck. "I dated his daughter Susan at one time," Bob said. "He was cordial but didn't beat about the bush. We had drinks while he explained the drawbacks of marriage. Fox had invested over two million dollars in Marilyn Monroe, and *Niagara* hadn't been released yet."

Zanuck did not have to mention that her contract was up for renewal. He merely said, "We want the public to think of Marilyn as the typical American blonde waiting to meet her Prince Charming, settle down and have a family." Zanuck remained friendly but threatened, "You could be blackballed in Hollywood, Marilyn. Undo what you did. That's it."

Marilyn and Bob left Zanuck's office and talked it over. Both were devastated, but they drove to Tijuana the following day. Bob bribed the attorney with fifty dollars to annul the marriage before finding out the paper, one of many jammed into a file cabinet, had yet to be filed.

"I'll destroy it," the lawyer said.

"No," Bob spoke up. "I want that paper!"

It occurred to him that the attorney might have recognized Marilyn and planned to use the document as blackmail. Finally the mangy lawyer lit a match and burned the paper in an oversized ashtray filled with stale cigarette butts. Marilyn sighed, "Well, there goes our marriage up in smoke."

Some of Monroe's friends think she eloped with Slatzer to escape DiMaggio, fearing a life of loneliness. But Bob believes the timing was all wrong. "A year earlier Zanuck would have ignored the whole thing," he said. "A year later Marilyn had the power to do as she pleased." In fact, both Slatzer and Marilyn regretted the annulment, according to reliable sources. She cried for days and was more confused and upset by Joe's repeated phone calls.

She was torn between two men, but Bob understood and supported Marilyn's career obsession whereas DiMaggio sought to protect her from the phony and blinding glitter of the spotlight. When she innocently told Joe he had no idea what it was like to have thousands of people stand up and applaud him, the Yankee Clipper replied humbly, "Seventy-five thousand. That's all." This was the seating capacity at Yankee Stadium. . . .

Marilyn continued to consult and rely on Bob Slatzer even though he married an auburn-haired girl from Ohio in 1954. After his divorce he endured a two-year stormy marriage to a blonde model from New Orleans, which ended in 1960.

Looking back, Slatzer believes that Marilyn would have been better off married to him and maintaining her friendship with DiMaggio instead of the other way around. And there are those who agree with Bob. But "What Should Have Been" is the story of Marilyn's life.

9

Joe

In 1953, Marilyn made the list of the Top Ten, an annual poll of movie exhibitors: Gary Cooper, Martin & Lewis, John Wayne, Alan Ladd, Bing Crosby, Marilyn Monroe, James Stewart, Bob Hope, Susan Hayward and Randolph Scott. Being one of only two women on the list was quite a feat for Marilyn, thanks to *Niagara*.

The *New York Herald-Tribune* said that Marilyn gave the kind of serpentine performance that made the audience hate her while admiring her. The *New York Times* review praised the scenic effects of Niagara Falls *and* Marilyn. "... Seen from any angle, the Falls and Miss Monroe leave little to be desired by any reasonably attentive audience. . . . Perhaps Miss Monroe is not the perfect actress at this point. But neither the director or the gentlemen who handled the cameras appeared to be concerned with this ... they have illustrated pretty concretely that she can be seductive—even when she walks. *Niagara* may not be the place to visit under these circumstances, but the Falls and Miss Monroe are something to see."

Marilyn was given star treatment at 20th Century-Fox. In comparison to the closet quarters she was accustomed to, the studio gave her a deluxe spacious dressing room. The reigning queen at Fox was Betty Grable, who had worn the crown for ten years and would soon relinquish it to her biggest fan, Marilyn Monroe.

Zanuck purchased the rights to *Gentlemen Prefer Blondes* at Grable's request. The details are sketchy as to whether he intended Betty to play the part of Lorelei Lee, the blonde gold-digger who sings, "Diamonds Are a Girl's Best Friend." Grable was holding her own at the box office after ten years of reaping in the profits for Fox, but Zanuck decided to give Monroe the part of Lorelei. Betty was furious but she told the press, "Any number of girls do what I do. After all, Mr. Zanuck and Mr. Schenck are the bosses."

Fox no longer needed Grable and she knew it. A professional to the end, she never lost her sparkle. She was a fine example for Marilyn who emulated Betty by studying her movies and talking to anyone who worked with the Pin-Up Girl. The two most famous blondes in the world became close friends before Grable bid farewell to Hollywood. They had more in common than either of them imagined.

Fox wanted Jane Russell for the part of Lorelei's sidekick Dorothy. They paid a tidy sum to borrow her from Howard Hughes, who had Jane under contract for twenty years, paying her $10,000 a week whether she worked or not. Zanuck did not quibble over the $500,000 loan-out fee for Russell. He could afford it since Marilyn was making only $500 a week. (Zanuck renewed her contract without a raise in pay.)

Hughes supervised Russell's career. She did not sing a song or wear a dress on screen without his approval. When she was loaned to Fox for *Gentlemen Prefer Blondes*, Hughes loaned out her crew from RKO, also. But Jane was not a Joan Crawford or Ava Gardner, who travelled with an entourage and primped their way through a film without having to pick up a powder puff. Russell was a great girl who worked hard, but took her career in stride.

Marilyn had to be reminded that Jane was the undisputed

star of *Gentlemen Prefer Blondes* and "... don't walk in front of Miss Russell on camera!" Jane and Marilyn became good friends and filming went well until director Howard Hawks threw Natasha Lytess off the set. Marilyn started coming to the set late. Rather than complain about it, Russell asked around and found out Marilyn was at the studio before anyone else, but afraid to report for work. From then on Jane called for Monroe every morning—"C'mon, Blondie, let's go!"

"Oh, okay," Marilyn replied, and they walked to the set together.

Joe DiMaggio came to the studio, and loud angry voices were heard coming from Marilyn's dressing room. She asked Jane Russell, whose husband was football hero Bob Waterfield, what it was like being married to an athlete.

"Well," Jane replied, "they're birds of a feather and you'll get to know lots of other athletes—otherwise, it's great." Russell and Waterfield were divorced in 1968 after twenty-five years of marriage.

Marilyn was adjusting once again to working without Natasha on the set. She was delighted with the musical numbers, especially "Diamonds Are a Girl's Best Friend." Choreographer Jack Cole said the original setting was Monroe in a great enormous Empire Bed, pale pink chiffon sheets and black satin cover. "She was wearing nothing but diamonds with a little horse's tail coming out of her ass with a little diamond horsefly on the tail."

They shot that number last, but by that time the studio had received thousands of letters from women's clubs complaining that Monroe's pictures were too flagrantly sexual. Zanuck cancelled the red and pink bedroom setting of "Diamonds Are a Girl's Best Friend." Cole said, "Marilyn almost had to go to the hospital when she heard we were not going to do the number this way."

The shocking pink gown that Marilyn wore in the final version was lined with felt to prevent the taffeta from clinging to her body. It was a magnificent dress that has gone down in history, but there is no Monroe cleavage and she wiggled within the confines of the wrap-around felt underneath.

Zanuck might have ignored the flood of scathing letters about Marilyn's lack of decorum, but he could not disregard the ugly publicity she was getting for showing up at the *Photoplay* Gold Medal Award dinner wearing a gown that looked as if it had been sprayed on her body. Columnist Sheila Graham said it was appalling.

Despite pleas from her closest friends and advisors, Marilyn wore a very low-cut gold lamé pleated gown with paper-thin lining hand-stitched to her nude curves. Master of Ceremonies Jerry Lewis stood up on a chair, trying to get a better look at her cleavage, although it was visible from any angle. The Crystal Room was in an uproar, and it got worse when Marilyn walked to the dais to accept her award for "Fastest-Rising Star of 1952."

Sheila Graham said, "Once you are a star, every door opens, everyone is rushing to kiss your rear and how Marilyn flaunted her rear end! In her public appearance gown you could see every crevasse. I had never seen anything like it in public. She was the living end."

Joan Crawford turned to Rock Hudson and Grace Kelly, who were sitting at her table, and hissed, "I had to work damn hard before I got that much attention. Today an artificial chin, a nose job and a bottle of peroxide's more important than talent and class."

The next day Joan talked to writer Bob Thomas. "Look, there's nothing wrong with my tits, but I don't go around throwing them into people's faces." Thomas wrote an article about his interview with Crawford: "It was a burlesque show. The publicity has gone too far, and apparently Miss Monroe is making the mistake of believing her publicity. Someone should make her see the light. She should be told that the public likes provocative feminine personalities, but it also likes to know that underneath it all the actresses are ladies. . . . "

Marilyn told Louella Parsons that she was hurt by the crowd's reaction. "I walked like a lady. And they all jumped on me. Why?"

Ouch.

In regard to Joan's comments, Marilyn told Parsons that she cried all night. "I've always admired Miss Crawford for being such a wonderful mother—for taking four children and giving them a fine home. Who better than I knows what that means to homeless little ones?"

But it seems that Crawford was verbally spanking Monroe for resisting her advances a few years earlier when Marilyn was living with the Kargers. Joan wanted to improve Marilyn's appearance and told her to try on several dresses from her expensive wardrobe. Joan said, "They're yours if they fit." Marilyn, who was taller and heavier, replied, "I wouldn't even attempt to squeeze into them, but thank you."

Joan wanted to see Marilyn's naked body and did not give up so easily. At a cocktail party she was slightly drunk and made a direct pass at Monroe who turned away: their friendship ended abruptly.

Crawford's bisexuality can only be verified by those women who responded, but her attempts are well known.

As for Monroe, she allowed Natasha Lytess to have her way if we are to believe what she told Lena Pepitone. But it was not a lingering sexual bond on her part. "Don't love me," she told Lytess, "just teach me."

In June of 1953, Marilyn Monroe and Jane Russell placed their hands and feet in wet cement on the sidewalk entrance to Graumann's Chinese Theater on Hollywood Boulevard. After they signed their names, Marilyn thought it would be cute if she left her fanny imprint and she told Jane Russell to lean forward so her breasts were etched in cement.

These ceremonies at Grauman's were memorable events that were limited to a few Hollywood stars. Russell said, "Marilyn and I were so thrilled!"

Marilyn found a three-room apartment on Doheny Drive. Until it was vacant and renovated, she moved into the luxurious Beverly Hills Hotel. DiMaggio filled her $750 suite with flowers and notes expressing his love, love, love. But when Joe was out of town, Marilyn had her share of lovers: Billy Travilla, who had designed her dresses at Fox for three years, Eddie Robinson, Jr., and Nicky Hilton (Elizabeth Taylor's first husband) were among them. She called Slatzer frequently in the wee hours. Her sleeping capsules never seemed to take effect until it was time to leave for the studio. To wake up, Marilyn took amphetamines, as did the majority of her peers in Hollywood. She had taken a variety of pills for years, but began abusing them now that the pressure was on.

Gentlemen Prefer Blondes was a smash. The *New York Times* might have been critical of Howard Hawks, but said, "... there is that about Miss Russell and also about Miss Monroe that keeps you looking at them even when they have little or nothing to do. Call it inherent magnetism. Call it coquetry. Call it whatever you fancy. . . . "

The *Herald-Tribune* called it THE HAYSTACK BRUNETTE VERSUS THE BLOWTORCH BLONDE: "Miss Monroe looks as though she would glow in the dark, and her version of the baby-faced blonde whose eyes open for diamonds and close for kisses is always amusing as well as alluring."

On the heels of *Gentlemen Prefer Blondes*, Fox planned to film *How to Marry a Millionaire* in CinemaScope, a new wide-screen process that Fox owned. (*Millionaire* was the first movie filmed in CinemaScope, but was released two months after *The Robe*, Fox's multimillion-dollar spectacular.) CinemaScope was an experiment for everyone. The actors had to keep moving and not be too close together because the screen was long and narrow.

How to Marry a Millionaire is the story of three models looking for rich husbands: Betty Grable as Loco, Lauren Bacall as Schatze, and Monroe as Pola. Bacall wrote in her memoirs that Marilyn was always late. During their scenes together she looked at Lauren's forehead instead of her eyes. At the end of each take, Marilyn looked to her coach for approval. If the headshake was no, she'd insist on another take. (When Natasha was fired, Marilyn refused to work, and Natasha was reinstated.)

The scene was done over and over. "I had to be good in all of them," Bacall said, "… not easy and often irritating. Yet I didn't dislike Marilyn. She had no meanness in her—no bitchery. Grable and I decided we'd try to make it easier on her, make her feel she could trust us. I think she finally did. She came to my dressing room one day and said that what she really wanted was to be in San Francisco with Joe DiMaggio in some spaghetti joint."

But Bacall was annoyed having to sit and wait on the set for Marilyn. Grable, who planned to tear up her Fox contract after *Millionaire*, said to Bacall, "It's her time. She's on her way up there as the biggest star. So let's not worry about it. I've got plenty of time. After all, they're paying me."

Grable and Monroe got along famously. When Betty had to rush home because her daughter was ill, she received a call that night. "Betty, how's Jessica?"

"She's okay. Who's this?"

"It's Marilyn …"

"Marilyn who?" Betty asked.

Lauren Bacall's cool and brainy Schatze in *Millionaire* was written with Bacall in mind. To the public and veterans of World War II, Betty Grable was the gal who preferred hot dogs and beer. But Marilyn had no character identity until screenwriter Nunnally Johnson made her nearsighted. Though she wasn't keen on wearing glasses, this was a blessing in disguise. Marilyn proved her ability as a comedienne, and erased some of the sex stigma that was working against her. She is adorable bumping into walls and reading a book upside down.

Marilyn wanted to attend the premiere of *How to Marry a Millionaire*, but DiMaggio refused to take her even though he was staying at her new apartment on Doheny Drive. Marilyn told Grable, "I'd rather not have another escort and I can't go alone."

"I'm not much for premieres," Betty said. "But this might be fun. Why don't we go together?"

Marilyn perked up. "Okay. It's a date."

"I'll pick you up, honey, but be on time."

The girls borrowed lavish gowns (Marilyn was sewn into a white lace creation), furs and diamonds from Fox wardrobe. Betty drove up in her Cadillac and the two most famous blondes in the world were off to the Hollywood premiere of *How to Marry a Millionaire* in November of 1953.

The reviews were excellent. Critics thought the movie was very entertaining, but they had just as much to say about the technical "bugs" of CinemaScope. The *New York Times* thought Miss Bacall was hardheaded, cold and waspish. "However, the baby-faced muggings of the famously shaped Miss Monroe does compensate in some measure for the truculence of Miss Bacall.

"Miss Grable, as the breezy huntress … is the funniest of the ladies."

Betty could leave Fox with her head held high. Marilyn inherited Grable's all-white dressing room, but refused to pose for publicity pictures when she moved into the royal chambers.

The Monroe-DiMaggio affair dragged on. Marilyn was learning to make his favorite Italian sauce and gleefully talked about dashing home to cook dinner for Joe. He remained adamant about not attending public functions with her, and word got around Hollywood that he was ashamed to be seen with Marilyn.

But Joe was intent upon marrying her. They were content away from the glare of Hollywood. Marilyn was a different person in

San Francisco, where Joe owned a modest house. She enjoyed getting up early and going fishing with him. He loved her with no makeup, wearing jeans or a simple dress, and sitting around the dinner table with his family. This was Joe's world. He believed it could be Marilyn's too. But she yearned for both worlds—the excitement of success, and a loving husband who wanted kids as much as she did.

DiMaggio proved how much he cared for Marilyn when she was on location in the Canadian Rockies filming *River of No Return* with Robert Mitchum. Angry at director Otto Preminger, Marilyn feigned an injury to her leg. X rays did not show any broken bones, but she wanted a cast "to be on the safe side."

Shelley Winters, filming nearby, was with Marilyn when the fake accident occurred. "Dumb? Like a fox, was my friend Marilyn," Shelley said.

DiMaggio and his doctor rushed to Marilyn's side. She kept up the charade and disappeared with Joe for a weekend. He stayed with her on location for a while and was friendly with everyone working on *River of No Return*, a film he considered "fairly" respectable. Marilyn was a saloon singer, but she spent most of her time on a raft with Mitchum, fighting the rapids and the Indians. (Once again Natasha was barred from the set. Marilyn put pressure on Zanuck, and Natasha was reinstated.)

Mitchum admired Monroe. He said in an interview, "Marilyn and I are a lot alike. There's not one single day when we can do one single thing completely gracefully. We're always in the soup."

About *River of No Return*, the *New York Post*'s movie critic said, "There is something at once incongruous and strangely stimulating in Miss Monroe's dazzled and dazzling antics in the surroundings of nature. She herself is a leading representative of the natural instinct mentioned previously. . . . "

The *New York Times* wrote, "It is a toss-up whether the scenery or the adornment of Marilyn Monroe is the feature of greater attraction in *River of No Return*. The mountainous scenery is spectacular, but so, in her own way, is Miss Monroe."

Twentieth Century-Fox announced that Marilyn's next film would be *Heller in Pink Tights*, with Frank Sinatra. Joe DiMaggio was indirectly responsible for her turning it down, citing the fact that Sinatra was making big money compared to what she was getting. As a result, Marilyn was suspended for six months. Joe convinced her to spend the Christmas holidays with his family in San Francisco. She seemed content with the DiMaggios and was thrilled to receive a mink coat from Joe. He was more thrilled that Marilyn was not depressed or concerned about being suspended. Ask ten close associates and they'll give you ten reasons why she married DiMaggio. Marilyn had a few versions, too. She said they suddenly decided two days before going through with it. She also gave the impression they had made up their minds before Christmas but the date wasn't set. Marilyn told Bob Slatzer she was confused. "When Joe and I got to city hall I remember asking, 'What are we doing here?' " There might be some merit to this since the couple obtained their marriage license and called Judge Peery only minutes before the ceremony. On the other hand, Marilyn was dressed for the occasion in a brown suit with an ermine collar.

On Saturday, January 14, 1954, at 1:45 P.M. in San Francisco City Hall, Monroe and DiMaggio took their wedding vows. He slipped a white gold wedding band with diamonds on her third finger, left hand.

By the time the newlyweds left city hall, a sizeable crowd had gathered. A reporter yelled to Joe, "What now?" The groom winked. "Whacha think?" In answer to the usual question about having babies, the groom said, "At least one." The bride said, "Lots."

As they were getting into Joe's car, he was overheard saying to his bride, "Let's forget about the reception and get outta here!"

They drove South to Pasa Robles, spent their wedding night at a cheap motel, and two weeks at a friend's cabin in the mountains near Palm Springs. Marilyn told a reporter that she and Joe were alone the whole time. "We didn't even have a TV set," she said with a half-smile. The rest of their honeymoon would be spent in Tokyo where DiMaggio was opening the official Japanese baseball season. When their plane stopped off in Hawaii to refuel, crowds at the airport chanted Marilyn's name. She barely made it in one piece to the lounge. DiMaggio must have known this demonstration was a hint of what to expect in Tokyo, but he was a hero to the Japanese, and their reception for him would make Marilyn proud.

"*Mon-chan! Mon-chan*," they cried at the airport in Tokyo. Four thousand Japanese were shouting for their "love child," an endearing term that hardly described the Yankee Clipper. Another mob of thousands were waiting at the Imperial Hotel. Three hundred policemen were required to keep the crowd in control. Marilyn satisfied their curiosity by waving to them from her balcony.

The DiMaggios had to cancel several press conferences to avoid overly enthusiastic crowds. A few articles described Joe as the "glowering husband." He went about his baseball business with a subdued Marilyn who kept a low profile, walking a few paces behind him. Away from the hub of Tokyo, the atmosphere was relatively calm.

At a cocktail party, Marilyn was approached by an Army officer who asked if she would fly over to Korea for a few days to entertain servicemen. Joe shook his head, but the officer emphasized how much the troops needed cheering up. "And we would be proud to have you, Mr. DiMaggio," he added. Joe had prior commitments in Japan, but he reluctantly said it was all right if Marilyn went alone. She claimed that the trip to Korea was the most wonderful experience of her life.

In sub-zero weather, Marilyn wore a low-cut clinging purple sequin dress on stage with nothing else on her body except high heels. It was quite a show! She sang "Diamonds Are a Girl's Best Friend," "Bye Bye Baby," and "Do It Again." For three days Marilyn ate in the mess hall with the boys, paraded around in army fatigues, and sang for them in a snowstorm, wearing her skimpy skin-tight gown. Needless to say, the worldwide publicity was sensational—and shocking.

But Marilyn could do nothing halfway. She could not perform for 100,000 young men without showing her body—in essence giving them everything she had. They were entitled to see the real Marilyn Monroe, and she wasn't going to let them down even though the temperature hovered around zero. Her phone conversations with Joe were just as cold.

Marilyn developed a high fever and was diagnosed as having a mild case of pneumonia. She flew back to Japan and was confined to bed for a week. Her illness undoubtedly prevented a violent argument with Joe, but the honeymoon trip to the Orient was the beginning of the end of their marriage.

10

Three Balls. Two Strikes.

Marilyn and Joe returned to his house in San Francisco. He spent a good deal of time at his restaurant on Fisherman's Wharf while she shopped and cooked. It was only natural that people patronizing DiMaggio's eatery would ask about Marilyn. He thought it would be a good idea if she had a meal there more than occasionally. This annoyed her and she purposely stayed home because, as she told a friend, "He's trying to use me."

Conversely, Joe was overheard advising Marilyn about her career: "Never mind about the publicity, honey. Just get the dough!"

Joe accused her of seeing other men (not yet) and being oversexed (she wasn't). He thought it vulgar if Marilyn sat around the house without clothes, but her nude presence did not prevent Joe from watching sports on TV. Nor was he in any hurry to get her into bed. There's no doubt that these little incidents added up to disaster, but in the sex department Marilyn never changed her opinion about Joe's prowess in bed. "He was the best equipped," she said. "The greatest. If our marriage was only sex it would last forever."

In March of 1954, Marilyn went to Hollywood to accept an award for "The Most Popular Actress." She and agent Charles

Feldman met with Zanuck to discuss her next film *There's No
Business Like Show Business* with Ethel Merman, Donald
O'Connor, Dan Dailey, Mitzi Gaynor and Johnnie Ray.
Marilyn was outclassed in this musical. She came across
without a glimpse of talent as an actress or singer. Her big
number was "Heat Wave," but Marilyn's costume was
unbecoming, her singing was dull and meaningless and her
dancing was obnoxious. Her skirt was open down the middle
and she was told to flap it between her legs, shake it apart and
spread her thighs and knees apart. "They said it was good for
me, good for the picture," Marilyn told her friends. "Shit!
Good for them, that's all. Everybody hated me after that
picture—including Joe. They wanted him to pose with me on
the set, but he wouldn't. The next day he was proud to pose
with Ethel Merman and Irving Berlin. He told me they
deserved to be stars because they had real talent."

Joe yelled at her, "Look at you and look at Ethel. What could
you do on a Broadway stage?"

Marilyn, in tears, said to her former lover and dress designer
Billy Travilla, "Every day I lose another piece of my mind." She
couldn't eat or sleep, looked like hell, and trembled on the set.
She was on the brink of a physical and mental breakdown.

According to Bob Slatzer, Zanuck stepped in, ordering
DiMaggio not only out of the studio but out of Marilyn's life,
and hired the best lawyer in the country to get her out of the
marriage. "DiMaggio had to resort to drastic measures,"
Slatzer said.

Natasha disliked Joe from the start. Now she had cause to
hate him, and the feeling was mutual. A sobbing Marilyn called
Natasha every night complaining about Joe's abusing her.
Rather than go home after work, Marilyn often stayed with
Natasha or spent the night at the studio. DiMaggio wanted to
get rid of Lytess for reasons other than her lesbianism. It was
Natasha who convinced Marilyn that she could be a great
actress, coaching and reassuring her with every passing day. Joe

finally told his famous wife to make a choice between him and her coach. Either Marilyn didn't take him seriously or didn't care because she continued to study with Natasha.

There's No Business Like Show Business got mixed reviews. Merman, Dailey and O'Connor could do no wrong, but Marilyn could do nothing right. Hedda Hopper's column tore her to shreds. Ed Sullivan wrote, "Miss Monroe has just about worn the welcome off this observer's mat. ... 'Heat Wave' is easily one of the most flagrant violations of good taste this observer has ever witnessed."

Bosley Crowther's review in the *New York Times* read: "... when it comes to spreading talent, Mitzi Gaynor has the jump on Miss Monroe whose wriggling and squirming to 'Heat Wave' and 'Lazy' are embarrassing to behold."

Marilyn's life during production of *Show Business* was in shambles. She went through the motions like a bored burlesque cutie. Knowing she could not compete with the other cast members, there was no glow in her eyes, no adorable smile and no enthusiasm or warmth. She had an affair with a young homosexual "... to make him feel good," she told a friend who refused to identify the man. It could have been Johnnie Ray or Dan Dailey. Marilyn was seen having dinner with both actors.

What comes to mind is Betty Grable's affair with Dailey, who was attracted to men even though he had a wife and children. Grable's husband, Harry James, caught Betty and Dan making love in her dressing room. Dailey ran for his life, leaving Grable behind to take the blame and the blows from Harry.

Betty invited Marilyn and Joe for dinner at her home. While James and DiMaggio discussed baseball, the girls talked about their abusive husbands. Grable would receive late night calls from a desperate Marilyn. "C'mon over," Betty yawned. "I know what it's all about, honey." Grable was crazy about Harry James, but after twenty-two stormy years, she divorced him on the grounds of extreme cruelty.

Marilyn and Joe were living in a house on North Palm Drive in fashionable Beverly Hills. The lease was in her name and, according to Slatzer, Marilyn paid the $800 a month rental. Joe did not feel the least bit responsible for anything that was related to his wife's career. As far as he was concerned, his home in San Francisco was their official address.

In the summer of 1954, Marilyn left Joe behind and flew to New York with Natasha to begin filming *The Seven Year Itch*. As the playful model subletting the apartment above Tom Ewell, whose wife is away for the summer, Marilyn is at her very best. She is delightful dipping potato chips in champagne and playing chopsticks on the piano while Ewell dreams of a passionate love affair.

The entire movie is grand, but the scene where Marilyn stands over a subway grating with her skirt blowing in the air is legend. Crowds gathered to watch rehearsals and repeated retakes of Marilyn, her legs apart, waiting for an air gush from the passing subway trains. Apparently, there was only one disgusted observer, Joe DiMaggio. He arrived in New York unexpectedly and, unfortunately, in time to see his wife enjoying herself while a thousand spectators cheered her on. Columnists Earl Wilson and Sidney Skolsky were standing near DiMaggio, who did not try to conceal his anger. Walter Winchell thought Joe's grunts and groans sounded more like sobbing than disgust before he left the scene. When Marilyn met him later, she tried to make light of the episode, but her battles with Joe were horrendous in New York. Other members of the cast had adjoining rooms at the St. Regis Hotel and heard yelling and loud commotions coming from the DiMaggio suite. Marilyn had the black and blue marks to prove how serious these bouts had become, but this was nothing new.

Marilyn was slightly heavier in *The Seven Year Itch*, but she carried the weight well because expectant mothers have that unexplained radiance. Author Sandra Shevey wrote that

Marilyn was pregnant and got an abortion at Cedars of Lebanon hospital when she returned to Los Angeles in late September. On October 3, 1954, Marilyn filed for divorce, accusing DiMaggio of mental cruelty. Even though they were still living under the same roof, Joe did not offer to face the press with her. Marilyn called her makeup man Whitey Snyder to come to the house. When he got there a swarm of reporters were on the front lawn, so he went in the backdoor and noticed that Joe was watching television in the living room. Whitey went upstairs and was startled to find Marilyn with two black eyes. Under the circumstances, he did a splendid job covering them up.

Marilyn emerged from the house with her attorney. A pathetic sight, she wept tears stained with mascara and wobbled in a faint. The only words she could manage were, "I'm sorry … there's nothing I can say. . . . " Reporters were anxious for the lowdown, but they were genuinely sorry for Marilyn, who broke down completely in the limousine.

A few minutes later Joe left the house and got into his car. "Where are you going?" a reporter asked.

"I'm going home," he replied. "San Francisco has always been my home."

On October 27, 1954, Marilyn testified in court that Joe was a cold loveless husband who did not speak to her for days, and how she was not allowed to have visitors. When Marilyn said she was under a doctor's care, the judge granted her an interlocutory decree of divorce.

To the amazement of those who knew her well, Marilyn began to blame herself for the breakup. "I was too busy," she lamented. "I should have come home earlier. Joe likes me to cook dinner. He was starved for attention."

Marilyn had begun seeing a psychiatrist and would continue to do so for the rest of her life. Guilt-ridden and confused by Joe's accusations that her sexual behavior was abnormal (including accusations of lesbianism), she sought help.

These few months in late 1954 were ones of defeat and triumph for her. There was the abortion and the divorce. But there was also a formal party given in her honor at Romanoffs after the completion of *The Seven Year Itch*. Fox said she could invite all her frends. Marilyn thought for a moment and only came up with Betty (Grable) and Harry James, and Lauren (Bacall) and Humphrey Bogart. It was a star-studded evening. Anybody who was anybody in Hollywood was there. It was there that Marilyn met her idol Clark Gable for the first time. "Golly, do you think he'll ask me to dance?" she sighed. Gable did not let her down. Since Marilyn came alone to her own party and Gable was between wives, there was speculation that they had a one-night stand. This is unlikely, but not from lack of desire on their part. Clark told Marilyn that he would like to make a picture with her. Six years later they would co-star in *The Misfits* but for the duration of a fox-trot at Romanoffs, Marilyn was in the arms of the man who resembled her father—the man whose picture she still carried in her pocketbook—Clark Gable.

Marilyn's attempts to see Stanley Gifford, whom she believed to be her father, failed. The third Mrs. Gifford said he even refused to come to the telephone. Natasha begged Marilyn not to contact him because "you'll only get hurt."

Marilyn had a father complex, referring to her husbands as "Daddy" or "Pa." She shocked friends by revealing her innermost fantasy: "Wearing a black wig, I make a date with my father, seduce him and then ask how it feels making love to his own daughter."

For twenty-eight years, Clark Gable indirectly played a vital role in Marilyn's life. When they were making *The Misfits*, he spent more time waiting for her than actually filming. Marilyn told Bob Slatzer, "I guess I was getting revenge on my father by punishing Gable. They were one and the same to me for as far back as I can remember. I wanted to please Clark more than anything, but took out my frustrations on him."

Gable had had more than his fair share of women and might

have given Marilyn a whirl, but the fifty-four-year-old King of Hollywood was tired. Recently he had struggled with himself over Grace Kelly, who resembled his beloved Carole Lombard, a plane-crash victim in 1942. Though the thirty-year age difference was a factor, Grace's career was just beginning, and Gable did not want to be a part of the rat race all over again. By the time he met Marilyn, Clark had proposed to Kay Spreckels, who would bear him a son after his death.

Life magazine wrote about the elaborate party given for Marilyn Monroe, noting in particular that The King had danced with the new Princess of Hollywood. The article, *"Life Goes to a Party,"* mentioned the impressive guest list that included the Zanucks, the Goldwyns, the Warners, Gary Cooper, George Burns and Gracie Allen, Susan Hayward, Loretta Young, the Jameses and the Bogarts, Clifton Webb, the William Holdens, Doris Day and the Jimmy Stewarts.

Frank Sinatra was resting up from the night before when he and Joe DiMaggio staged the now-famous "Wrong Door Raid," in an attempt to catch Marilyn with another man. Slatzer thinks Joe was after proof that she was having a lesbian affair. "It was the same thing as blackmail," Bob said. "If Joe D. had the evidence, he'd use it to get Marilyn back."

On the night of November 5, 1954, DiMaggio met Sinatra at the Villa Nova, an Italian restaurant. When they received a call from detective Barney Ruditsky—who had been hired by Joe several months before to follow Marilyn—saying that he'd spotted her parked car, Joe and Frank left in a rush and joined Ruditsky in front of an apartment house on the corner of Waring Avenue and Kilkea Drive in Beverly Hills. At 11:15 P.M., they broke down the door of an apartment rented, supposedly, by Marilyn's girlfriend, Sheila Stewart. When the lights went on, fifty-year-old Florence Kotz screamed as flash bulbs popped. The landlady saw a tall man, Joe, and a short man, Frank, running to their cars.

Marilyn was in Stewart's apartment directly above. Everyone

in the building was roused (and frightened) by the door crashing to the floor, loud voices and the screams of poor Mrs. Kotz. Marilyn peeked through the window and saw Joe's car zooming off in the darkness.

Anthony Summers, author of *Goddess: The Secret Lives of Marilyn Monroe*, wrote that vocal coach Hal Schaefer was with Marilyn at Stewart's place on that eventful night, and that they had been lovers for some time. It was not a serious affair and had no bearing on her divorce. Schaefer told Summers how he tried to commit suicide four months before the Wrong Door Raid. He does not cite Marilyn as the reason he took pills with brandy and cleaning fluid, but he does intimate that being constantly tailed by Joe's detectives, drove him over the edge. Miraculously, Schaefer survived and Marilyn stood by him during his touch-and-go recovery.

Journalist James Bacon remembered seeing Sinatra and DiMaggio arguing at the Villa Nova on the night of November 5. After they left, Hank Sanicola, Sinatra's manager, told Bacon, "Joe thinks Marilyn is shacked up with some guy who works on her pictures. He wants to break in on her, and Frank's been trying to talk him out of it."

Marilyn saw Bacon a few days later and laughed. "Joe is such a gentleman. Who else but a gentleman would kick in the wrong door?" But Bacon suspected Sinatra deliberately misled Joe to spare Marilyn. "Frankie thought it was a big joke," she said. "Joe didn't, and he blamed Frankie for messing things up. They had a fight and that was the end of their friendship." The fact that Sinatra began to date Marilyn enraged DiMaggio, but Marilyn shrugged that off, too. "Italian men are hard to figure out," she said.

Regarding the Wrong Door Raid, Slatzer added two very interesting revelations. "Ruditsky always carried a gun," he said, "and maybe Sinatra was afraid someone might get hurt. I also found out that Joe D. came to see Marilyn later that night. What they discussed, I don't know."

The Wrong Door Raid was hushed up until 1957 when Mrs. Kotz sued Ol' Blue Eyes and the Yankee Clipper. They settled out of court for $7,500.

Despite their divorce, Marilyn saw Joe frequently. "I never loved any guy more," she said, "but he resented my career and refused to compromise."

11

New York

The part of burlesque chorine Curly Flagg, in *How to Be Very, Very Popular*, was written with Marilyn in mind, but she refused to do it. No more dumb-blonde roles for her! She wanted to break away from Fox and change her image by doing serious parts. To avoid legal entanglements with the studio, Marilyn went in hiding at Frank Sinatra's place until he got fed up wth her walking around nude in front of his friends. She stayed with Anne Karger (Fred's mother) and then Marilyn secretly boarded a plane for New York shortly before the holidays.

Her travelling companion was a thirty-three-year-old photographer, Milton Greene. Marilyn had been introduced to him by Sammy Davis, Jr., at a cocktail party eighteen months before when Greene was in Hollywood taking pictures for *Look* magazine. Marilyn and Milton became good friends and, according to her, lovers as well. When he talked about plans to set up his own production company, she asked Greene to look over her Fox contract. He told Marilyn she was not getting the roles or the money she deserved.

When she was in New York to film scenes for *The Seven Year Itch*, Marilyn relied on Milton and his wife Amy after DiMaggio went on a rampage following the "skirt blowing" incident over the subway grating. The Greenes extended an invitation to their

Connecticut home, but it was not until after the divorce and Fox pressuring Marilyn to do *How to Be Very, Very Popular*, that she fled Hollywood. For almost a year and a half, she and Milton had been discussing the possibility of setting up Marilyn Monroe Productions. As president, she would own 51 per cent of the shares and, as vice president, Greene would own 49 per cent.

In hiding at the Greenes' country house, Marilyn refused to take phone calls in her attempt to avoid any legal action that 20th Century-Fox might take.

Since Marilyn was almost broke and without an income, Greene paid her expenses. Indirectly, he was investing his money in a sound commodity.

In January of 1955, Greene arranged a cocktail reception for the press at his lawyer's plush Manhattan apartment on East 64th Street to announce his partnership in Marilyn Monroe Productions. She told the press, "I'm tired of sex roles." Wearing a tight strapless satin dress with a full length ermine wrap, Marilyn proceeded to tell amused reporters how much she wanted to play Grushenka in *The Brothers Karamazov*. A reporter, trying to keep a straight face, asked her how to spell the names. "How would I know?" she replied.

Marilyn's toting Dostoevski's book under her arm was now a big joke in show business. The public thought it was a publicity campaign to prove that she was a versatile actress.

A spokesman for Fox said the studio had no intention of casting Marilyn in *The Brothers Karamazov*. Hollywood insiders laughed, but New Yorkers had a more sophisticated attitude. At a time when theater tickets were not expensive and Broadway shows were classics, people made a concerted effort to see every one of them. City dwellers thrived on concerts, ballet, opera and museums. Two of the finest acting schools were in Manhattan—The American Academy of Dramatic Arts and the Actors Studio. Though some of the students hoped to break into films, they were trained for the stage. While Hollywood snickered at

Marilyn, the Manhattan crowd admired her for literally giving up a dazzling career in an attempt to better herself.

Greene wanted Marilyn to maintain a glamorous image and star status, however. He paid for her expensive clothes, regular visits to the hairdresser and a new car. He arranged for her to ride a pink elephant at a Madison Square Garden benefit, and the crowd went wild. Whatever she did and wherever she went, Monroe was a sensation with or without Greene. He might have done her an injustice by booking a guest appearance on Edward R. Murrow's "Person to Person" from his Connecticut home. There were few movie stars who did not tremble at the very thought of live TV. Viewing the show today, Marilyn came across well, but seemed overshadowed by the presence of Milton and his poised wife, Amy. The first questions that came to mind were, "Who are those people and what is Marilyn Monroe doing there?"

Marilyn's faithful friends in Hollywood were disturbed by her business relationship with Greene. Natasha Lytess thought her former student was being manipulated and ill-advised. Bob Slatzer said Marilyn was well aware that Greene was using her, but she took advantage of him to escape an impossible situation at Fox. Others think she left Hollywood to get away from DiMaggio. This might have been the case following the Wrong Door Raid, but they were together again in the spring of 1955.

Marilyn moved into a suite at the Waldorf Astoria Hotel to be near the Actors Studio, where she hoped to study with its founder, Lee Strasberg. This was part of the master plan, financed by Greene's dwindling bank account.

DiMaggio was seen going in and out of Monroe's Waldorf suite regularly. Was there a chance of a reconciliation? Marilyn told a reporter they were very good friends, but Joe left the door open. He was trying to win her back before their divorce was final. Proof of this was his accompanying Marilyn to the New York premiere of *The Seven Year Itch* on June 1, her twenty-ninth birthday. Joe braved a smile despite the forty-foot poster of Marilyn with a wind-blown skirt dominating Times Square. Afterward, they attended a party he had arranged for her at Toots Shor. During the festivities, they argued and Marilyn walked out. He tried unsuccessfully to patch things up. These were precious months to DiMaggio. If the divorce became final, he knew Marilyn would never remarry him. Joe was a tormented man who tried breaking down her door and begging friends to intercede on his behalf. Marilyn finally made up her mind not to see Joe for a while.

The Seven Year Itch was a hit. The *New York Mirror* said that Marilyn was a fine comedienne.

The *New York Times*'s critic wrote, "... She [Monroe], without any real dimensions, is the focus of attention in the film. Thus, it is that the undisguised performance of Miss Monroe, while it may lack depth, gives the show a caloric content. . . . We merely commend her diligence when we say it leaves much—very much—to be desired."

Whatever damage had been done to Marilyn by her red hot musical numbers in *There's No Business Like Show Business*, was quickly repaired by *The Seven Year Itch*. Her performance opposite Tom Ewell overshadowed everything else she had done on the screen. It was a professional rebirth, and thousands of moviegoers sent fan letters to Marilyn at Fox. Zanuck had no choice but to renegotiate her contract that was signed on New Year's Eve of 1955. She would be committed to do four films during the next seven years, and was free to make one film a year for other studios. Fox agreed to pay Marilyn Monroe Productions $100,000 and a percentage of the profits for each film. Marilyn had the right to reject scripts that were not first class and to choose her own directors.

No one was more relieved than Milton Greene, who had been borrowing money to support Marilyn. She was not a spendthrift in the truest sense of the word, rather a little girl who had no conception of a dollar's value.

Shortly before her new deal with Fox, Marilyn had another

offer. Would she like to meet Prince Rainier of Monaco?

"Who?" she asked Gardner Cowles, publisher of *Look* magazine, a friend of Milton Greene's.

"The Prince of Monaco."

"Where's Monaco?" Marilyn asked. (A logical question since Grace Kelly's mother didn't know either. She thought her daughter was moving to Morocco!)

Cowles said Rainier was visiting the U.S., and rumor had it he was looking for a wife. Unless the prince produced an heir, Monaco would become part of France. Aristotle Onassis, who was concerned about his investments in Monte Carlo's Casino, wanted Rainier to get married. Naturally, it would help the economy if he chose a wealthy or famous bride.

"Would you like to meet the Prince?" Cowles asked Marilyn.

"Sure!" She giggled. "Give me two days alone with him and of course he'll want to marry me."

But a few days later the Philadelphia Kellys announced the engagement of their daughter Grace to Prince Rainier—and the rest is history. Few people realized how close he came to considering the possibility of "Princess Marilyn" sharing his throne.

Sheila Graham wrote in her column that Marilyn called Grace, whom she'd never met. "Congratulations. I really envy you getting out of this business."

If we are to believe Marilyn's casual statement to a friend that one of the reasons she came to New York was to pursue Arthur Miller, it is unlikely she had any interest in Prince Rainier other than out of curiosity.

Though Miller's fifteen-year marriage had been shaky for quite a while, he had no plans to divorce his wife. But neither he nor Marilyn could forget the attraction to one another when they had met in 1950. She felt the chemistry right away and was determined to see the playwright again. They corresponded over the years, and he was one of the few people who knew that Marilyn was coming to New York.

*

Arthur Miller was born on October 17, 1915, in New York City. He worked his way through the University of Michigan and won a drama award in his sophomore year. His first successful Broadway play was *All My Sons* in 1947, directed by Elia Kazan, one of Marilyn's former lovers.

In 1949, Miller became a highly respected playwright after he won the Pulitzer Prize for *Death of a Salesman*. He did not, however, stray far from his Jewish roots in Brooklyn, where he lived with his wife and two children.

Miller was not a rich man, nor was he particularly interested in money other than having enough to live comfortably. Tall and thin, with a craggy unsmiling face, Miller was friendly but quiet, and a loner whose success as a writer did not come easily. Miller said candidly that he had to work harder than most writers, and he required total concentration to accomplish anything worthwhile. For this reason alone he was not an easy person to live with.

The great attraction between Miller and Monroe was similar to the magnetism she shared with DiMaggio. Both men were unlikely candidates for marriage to a woman who needed constant attention and affection. But the physical bonds were overwhelming—and not entirely for the obvious reasons. Marilyn was sensitive, childlike, cuddly and clinging. When she wore a simple cotton afternoon dress, there was the freshness of youth and purity about her. A natural breathless quality in her voice was appealing, and reflected the vulnerability and fear that was buried in her soul. This was the Marilyn that Joe wanted to possess, and the Marilyn that completely captivated Miller. Her goal was to bring the playwright to his knees with a marriage proposal. Mutual friends who invited them to dinner were aware of the relationship and made it possible for the couple to see each other frequently without alerting the press. Miller was completely enchanted by Marilyn, but he was not one to rush into anything as serious and costly as divorce. In the meantime he concentrated on proving his devotion, love and loyalty.

Marilyn was not faithful to Arthur, however. She had an affair with Marlon Brando, who was also attending the Actors Studio in the summer of 1955. The thirty-one-year-old bachelor had been involved with many women, including Shelley Winters, but it was Mexican starlet Movita Castenada who knocked Marlon for a loop in 1951. Their stormy relationship continued during his affair with Marilyn, who was drawn to the actor *and* the man. She admired his rebellious attitude toward Hollywood labelled by him as a "cultural boneyard."

In 1947 Brando gained recognition on Broadway in *A Streetcar Named Desire*, with Jessica Tandy. He re-created the part of Stanley Kowalski on the screen with Vivien Leigh and was nominated for an Oscar. He did not win for *Streetcar* or *Viva Zapata!*, but walked away with the award for his third film directed by Elia Kazan—*On the Waterfront*. Brando was nominated again for his portrayal of Mark Antony in *Julius Caesar* (1953).

Brando was blunt about making movies only for the money but his sullen sex appeal and nonchalant hippie image was magnetic. He attracted a loyal cult that admired his insolence toward Hollywood. "Acting is the expression of a neurotic impulse," he said. "It is a bum's life. Quitting acting is a sign of maturity."

Marilyn's affair with Brando was intense but he lacked the maturity that she needed for a lasting relationship. He was an interesting interlude because she admired him immensely as an actor. As for Brando, he preferred dark-haired Asian- and Latin-type beauties like Movita, France Nuyen and Rita Moreno. Though he had little respect for women, there was a vulnerability about Marilyn that brought out whatever warmth he was capable of giving. She spoke of him as a gentle caring man, and he became a steadfast friend who refuses to discuss their relationshp to this day.

*

Brando returned to Hollywood in October 1955 and fell madly in love with Anna Kashfi when he spotted her in Paramount's commissary. Supposedly she was an Indian girl born in Calcutta, but the press revealed otherwise. Gossip columnist Sheila Graham wrote, "Miss Kashfi's parents were Welsh. She is about as Indian as Paddy's Pig."

It didn't matter to Brando that Anna fibbed about her past because she was an exquisite woman. The fact that she'd never heard of him was almost as tantalizing as the lady herself. In 1957, Marlon married Anna, and seven months later she gave birth to a son, Christian.

Marilyn's affair with Brando was well timed. She was distancing herself from Hollywood, but not without a good deal of fear. Marlon thrived on rebelling, but the major studios were willing to meet his demands. He and Marilyn were dedicated to the Actors Studio and what the Golden Era stars detested—Method acting, the art of "getting into the role and living it." Joan Crawford said, "It's a bunch of crap." Clark Gable felt the same way. He had to grind his false teeth waiting for a Method player "to get into the mood." The biggest stars of Hollywood considered Spencer Tracy the best actor of them all. "Spence had a formula," Gable said. "Get to the set on time, know your lines, don't fall over anything, and go home at six o'clock."

But these screen legends were being replaced by Method players and though Marilyn was a natural comedienne, she followed the likes of Shelley Winters, Marlon Brando and Elia Kazan. With Natasha Lytess out of her life, she turned to Paula and Lee Strasberg at the Actors Studio for guidance. To the amazement of everyone in her class, Marilyn proved she could handle serious parts fairly well. Moviegoers saw a smidgen of this in *Bus Stop*, for which she was acclaimed, but without her exposing her luscious body in several scenes, loyal fans would have been very disappointed.

Though Marilyn's decision to live in New York came about, ostensibly, to concentrate on improving her skills as an actress, she was just, if not more, anxious to be near Arthur Miller. Some of Marilyn's biographers claim she married him on the rebound after her affair with Brando. It would be more accurate to say she was biding her time until Miller announced his pending divorce. He did so in January of 1956, but there was no mention of Marilyn. The lovers had yet to be seen together in public and wanted to keep their relationship a secret for a while longer.

When Marilyn left New York in March to make *Bus Stop* in Hollywood, she hoped to be Mrs. Arthur Miller before the year's end.

12

Arthur

Marilyn had one more ace up her sleeve before facing those disbelievers in Tinseltown who considered her just another dumb blonde. On February 9, 1956, in the Terrace Room of New York's plush Plaza Hotel, she and Sir Laurence Olivier announced their plans to co-star in the film version of Terence Rattigan's *The Sleeping Prince*.

Marilyn wore a low-cut form-fitting black velvet cocktail sheath and matching coat. About the distinguished British actor who sat beside her she said breathlessly, "My hope and dream was to have him not only star but also direct."

Two hundred reporters looked at Sir Laurence for a statement. With little enthusiasm he said, "I was very interested in doing the film when the offer came."

When asked how his actress-wife Vivien Leigh felt about Marilyn playing the part she had done with him on stage, Olivier replied, "My wife never wanted to do the film."

"I own it," Marilyn interrupted sweetly but firmly.

Sir Laurence forced a smile and said, "The part of a young American chorus girl is not suitable for my wife in the film, although she was lovely on stage. She's a beautiful actress."

"I hope we produce the movie in London." Marilyn beamed. "I've never been to Europe."

During the interview, reporters asked Olivier to put his arm around Marilyn, but he ignored the request. When they begged her to bend over for more cleavage, she obliged until Sir Laurence suggested, "No more leg pictures, boys. From now on she's too ethereal."

When Marilyn began fiddling with a broken shoulder strap, reporter Judith Crist came to the rescue with a safety pin. This incident was the highlight of the press conference, of course, and annoying to Olivier who had already contended with Marilyn's being an hour late arriving at the Plaza. Then he was literally pushed aside until they were seated together in the Terrace Room where the press was not only treated to extra cleavage, but a broken shoulder strap as well!

When Marilyn's dress was repaired and everyone in the room waited for the safety pin to pop open, a reporter asked Sir Laurence what he thought about a recent statement that Marilyn had more sex appeal than any other actress in the world. He thought for a moment and then replied, "In my opinion, Miss Monroe has an extremely … uh … extra-ordinary—uh … gift of being able to suggest one moment that she is the naughtiest little thing and the next that she's perfectly innocent. The audience leaves the theater gently titillated into a state of excitement by not knowing which she is and enjoying it thoroughly."

About this time, Marilyn's dress strap was giving way again. Olivier called an end to the conference while she clutched her coat in front. As she proceeded to the ladies' room, a reporter asked, "Are you going to play *The Brothers Karamazov?*"

"I don't want to play the *Brothers*," she exclaimed. "I want to play Grushenka. She's a girl!"

Sir Laurence Olivier said he had been very anxious to meet Marilyn Monroe, but almost lost his patience before their initial introduction at her Sutton Place apartment that she sublet in the fall of 1955. Milton Greene was a congenial host, but when she failed to appear, Olivier wailed at her bedroom door, "For the love of God, hurry up, Marilyn. We're dying of anxiety!"

Several minutes after she walked in the room, Sir Laurence was sitting on the floor at her feet. "I don't recall a single word that was said," he admitted. "But one thing was clear to me. I was going to fall most shatteringly in love with Marilyn. She was so adorable, so witty and more physically attractive than anyone I could have imagined."

But Olivier was in for a bitter disappointment.

When Marilyn's plane landed in Los Angeles, a crowd of cheering fans and eager reporters were waiting. This reception was one of her greatest triumphs. She had won the battle with 20th Century-Fox and saved her production company from financial ruin.

The press said it was a "new Marilyn" who waved to fans and talked to reporters for nearly two hours at the airport. Travelling with Marilyn were the Greenes and Paula Strasberg, who remained in the background but near enough to be identified and photographed. They posed as Marilyn's saviors, but the change in Marilyn was of her own doing. She was more in charge of who and what she was than ever before. Though Arthur Miller was not involved in her career as yet, she had his support. While waiting for his divorce in Nevada, he called her every night, using the code name "Mr. Leslie."

In *Bus Stop* Marilyn plays the part of Cherie, a floosy singer with a questionable past, who captivates a young naive cowboy. She copied Cherie's indiscretions off-camera by seeing other men despite her love for Miller. Reportedly, she fired a publicity girl who flirted with her escort. Marilyn's deep insecurity at this time was mistaken for bad temperament on the movie set.

Concerned that Hope Lange's hair was too light in *Bus Stop*, Marilyn insisted the color be darkened so as not to distract from her own blonde image.

Then there was the matter of casting Rock Hudson as the shy

cowhand in the film. He was very interested in the part, but Marilyn gave into her fear that Hudson might steal the picture. She hesitated and then changed her mind too late. Hudson was committed to another project.

It was newcomer Don Murray who was chosen instead. He had had only bit parts in two movies—*Blood on the Moon* (1948) and *Dallas* (1951). Director Joshua Logan saw something in Murray and hoped *Bus Stop* would establish the young actor's career in films. Marilyn was upset over not signing Rock Hudson when she had the chance and took it out on Murray by swiping him viciously across the face with her beaded costume. Instead of faking the scene, Marilyn relied too heavily on the realism of Method acting. Murray stormed off the set and she refused to apologize.

Logan was plagued by Marilyn's bad temperament and tardiness, but took everything in his stride—everything, that is, except Paula Strasberg, who was determined to sit by the camera and direct Marilyn, defying Logan's instructions. He banned Strasberg from the set, but as she had done with Natasha, Marilyn disappeared between takes to confer with Paula. Logan got the results he wanted despite the bickering and delays. He understood Marilyn and kept the camera rolling even if she forgot her lines. More than once he went to her dressing room, took Marilyn firmly by the hand and told her to walk through scenes that required no dialogue.

Logan said that Monroe was the most exciting actress he had ever worked with, and whatever she did off-camera did not interest him. *Bus Stop* received excellent reviews. The toughest critic of them all, Bosley Crowther, wrote in the *New York Times*: "Hold on to your chairs, everybody, and get set for a rattling surprise. Marilyn Monroe has finally proved herself an actress in *Bus Stop*. . . ."

The *New York Herald-Tribune* said, "One minute it [*Bus Stop*] is uproariously funny, the next minute tender and fragile, and somehow director Josh Logan preserves the delicate balance."

Marilyn expected an Academy Award nomination for *Bus Stop*, but the chosen few were Carroll Baker in *Baby Doll*, Katharine Hepburn for *The Rainmaker*, Nancy Kelly in *The Bad Seed*, Deborah Kerr in *The King and I*, and Ingrid Bergman, who won the Best Actress award for *Anastasia*.

Bus Stop had stiff competition, also. Nineteen fifty-six was a year of great films: *The Ten Commandments*, *Giant*, *Lust for Life*, and *Gentle Persuasion*. It was the year that Elizabeth Taylor married Mike Todd, who jumped out of his seat to collect the Oscar for *Around the World in Eighty Days* but ran back up the aisle to kiss his bejeweled wife first. And it was the year that Hollywood welcomed back Ingrid Bergman with an Oscar tribute after her years of exile in Europe. She proved to be a survivor despite rumors and scandal, as did Elizabeth Taylor. Both actresses held their heads high through it all.

Marilyn was too fragile for the slings and arrows aimed at her, as many news film clips have revealed. By exposing her tortured soul to the public as she did on the day her divorce from Joe DiMaggio was announced, we saw clearly the pathetic and helpless aura of Marilyn. It was the combination of lonely frightened child and self-assured sex goddess that was so appealing not only to her fans, but to the men who fell in love with her.

Arthur Miller was aware of Marilyn's vulnerability and he tried to ease her through the tension of *Bus Stop*, but he had his own problems during those six weeks in Nevada. There were touchy divorce negotiations and though his wife was cooperative, she demanded a fair settlement. He was also served with a subpoena from the House Un-American Activities Committee to appear in Washington on June 21, 1956, to answer questions about his Communist affiliations, if any.

Though Miller told reporters he didn't "have a clue" as to why the committee summoned him, he faced a dilemma of naming names or being cited for contempt of court. Miller had previously admitted he supported an organization that had Communist connections, but denied being a member of the party. Nonetheless, he was denied a passport in 1954.

On June 12, the *New York Post* ran an article entitled ACT I: DEATH OF AN INTERVIEW. "The scene is Idlewild Airport at 8:05 A.M. The United Airlines flight from San Francisco throttles to a halt. Enter Arthur Miller, fashionable young Broadway playwright.

Reporter: Are you going to marry Marilyn Monroe?
Miller: No comment.
Reporter: We only bother you about this because people want to know.
Miller: It's your job versus my privacy. That's a remorseless conflict.
(Curtain)

Marilyn had returned to New York on June 3, two days after her thirtieth birthday. She arrived at 8:00 A.M. at Idlewild Airport and, as one reporter wrote, "Marilyn was at her seductive best—sleepy-eyed from the overnight flight from Hollywood and tempting in a tight black dress."

Marilyn avoided questions about Miller and sighed, "I'm suffering from fatigue. My doctor wants me to rest for a few weeks before leaving for England to work with Sir Laurence."

A reporter asked how it felt to be thirty years old. Marilyn yawned. "In Dr. Alfred Kinsey's opinion, a woman doesn't get started until she's thirty. That's good news and and it's supposed to be factual, too."

When the press asked her for "some cheesecake," she hitched up her skirt and pouted à la Monroe.

It doesn't seem possible that Arthur had not formally proposed marriage to Marilyn as yet. That he kept her informed of his divorce proceedings every night over the telephone was an indication of nothing more than wanting his freedom to be seen with her in public. Marilyn's nervousness and irritability during *Bus Stop* can be partially attributed to her not knowing if Arthur was seriously considering a permanent relationship. Was she good enough for the six-foot-two, forty-year-old intellectual playwright who had fame *and* stature? Marilyn wasn't sure.

Arthur was aware of her emotional problems, but he had no concept of how deep-rooted and life-threatening they were. He saw the little girl, not the tortured woman. Miller rarely discussed Marilyn after he discovered the hard way that dainty rosebuds have prickly thorns. Years later, he said, "If I had known how we would end up," he said, "I would never have married her."

Shakespeare wrote, "... love is blind, and lovers cannot see the pretty follies that themselves commit." And so Arthur Miller, one of the most unlikely candidates for the husband of Marilyn Monroe, chose to sacrifice his privacy and his wife of fifteen years for an enigma.

In June of 1956, there was much more at stake, however. The investigation into Miller's political leanings meant a possible jail sentence and the end of his career as a writer. For nearly a decade the House Un-American Activities Committee had questioned everyone, writers in particular, who were suspected of supporting the Communist party. Some went to jail, and many left the country because they refused to testify. Writer Carl Foreman— whose movie scripts included *Champion*, *Home of the Brave*, *Cyrano de Bergerac* and *High Noon*—was blacklisted in 1951 and forced to live in England, writing under an assumed name.

Right-wingers protested Miller's 1947 Pulitzer prize winning drama, *All My Sons*, and picketed the film version of *Death of a Salesman*. In 1953 his play *The Crucible*, about the Salem witch trials, appeared to echo Washington's ongoing "witch hunt" for Communists.

But Miller was not summoned to testify until his highly publicized involvement with Marilyn Monroe. Seeing the playwright's name in the newspaper almost daily was a constant reminder to members of the House Un-American Activities Committee that he had never been subpoenaed. Some journalists hinted a lull in the Congressional hearings prompted the Committee to get some much-needed publicity.

The reasons why are not important because Miller faced the same penalties as his fellow writers in past years. And there was proof that some of his friends were left-wingers and that he considered joining the party in 1943 though Miller claimed he did not fill out the unsigned membership card.

Before the hearing on June 21, 1956, Marilyn met Arthur's parents, who were surprised when their son introduced the stunning blonde wearing a simple blouse and skirt as "the girl I want to marry." It was a very emotional few minutes, especially for Marilyn who hugged and kissed the Millers. "At last I have a mother and father," she sobbed.

Those close to Marilyn warned her that Arthur's testimony might ruin her career. 20th Century-Fox was adamant that Miller cooperate with the Committee; the Strasbergs agreed. Marilyn, however, begged him *not* to name names. She would stand by him.

There had yet to be an official announcement of their pending marriage, but Marilyn did not try to hide her presence in Washington on June 21, 1956. Staying at the home of friends, she walked out on the front lawn and talked to a small group of reporters. "I believe he will win," she said with a smile.

Miller appeared calm when asked to give the names of persons who supported organizations linked to the Communist party. He told the Committee he understood their position, but he hoped they would understand his: "... the life of a writer, despite what it sometimes seems, is pretty tough. I wouldn't make it any tougher for anybody. I ask you not to ask me that question. I will tell you anything about myself, as I have."

When asked why he wanted a passport to go to England, Miller dropped a bombshell: "I have a production, which is in the talking stage in England, of *A View from the Bridge*, and I will be there with the woman who will then be my wife. That is my aim."

Marilyn heard about it and called a friend, shrieking with delight. "He told the whole world he was marrying Marilyn Monroe. Me! Can you believe it? You know he never really asked me!"

Columnist Hedda Hopper, a staunch right-winger, thought Miller used Marilyn: "That was a rotten way to make the announcement. He wasn't in any rush to get married until his back was against the wall."

Monroe's publicist Rupert Allan told author Sandra Shevey, "If Miller was such a prince, how do you explain that he would go to Washington and announce to the press that he and Marilyn were engaged without ever having asked her? If you need to marry anybody and you need to get back into the public image, why not marry the all-American girl?"

Miller took his contempt citation through the appellate courts. In 1958, it was concluded that he had not been duly informed of his rights and the charges were dropped.

In the meantime, his passport was renewed for six months instead of the customary two years.

Marilyn had no idea that she was being investigated by the FBI because of Miller, her friendships with the Strasbergs and others closely associated with the party. As for Communists she said, "They're for the people, aren't they?"

13

Mrs. Miller and Sir Laurence

Reporters were waiting outside Marilyn's Sutton Place apartment at 444 East 57th Street when she and Miller returned from Washington. The couple made a getaway in a station wagon with the press in fast pursuit all the way to Arthur's seventeenth-century farmhouse in Roxbury, Connecticut. When it became apparent that newsmen planned to camp on the grounds until they got a story, Miller promised them a press conference on Friday, June 29, at the farm.

Arthur's parents, Isadore and Augusta, spent the next few days in Roxbury, also. Marilyn learned to cook her future husband's favorite Jewish food, watching and tasting Augusta's borscht, chopped liver and matzoh balls. But it was a shock to the Miller family when Marilyn announced that she was converting to the Jewish faith. Rabbi Robert Goldberg gave her instructions in the Reformed branch of Judaism and asked that she study the Torah on her honeymoon.

Marilyn made this decision without any prompting. In private Isadore asked her, "Are you very sure?" She hugged him and whispered, "Very." Though Arthur was not a religious man, he was proud that Marilyn had elected to do this.

In the sweltering heat of Friday, June 29, 1956, hundreds of

reporters and photographers swarmed around the unpretentious nine-room "farmhouse" in Roxbury. Knowing Marilyn's
reputation for being late, no one expected her to show up at one
P.M. But several minutes before the appointed hour, a green
Oldsmobile appeared. Arthur Miller got out and made a mad
dash for the house with Marilyn running up the hill behind him.
Arthur's cousin Morton Miller remained in the car briefly, as if
in shock. He told newsmen, "There's been a terrible accident.
We were being followed by a white car that crashed on a sharp
turn. A woman has been seriously injured." (Myra Sherhatoff,
American correspondent for *Paris-Match* magazine, died in the
hospital.)

Arthur and Marilyn saw the accident and stopped to help.
When Marilyn rushed to the house, the blood of Miss
Sherhatoff was visible on her clothes. Marilyn was hysterical,
but calmed by the Millers in preparation for the press
conference. Arthur was more upset by the reporters who waited
like hungry vultures while the wailing siren of an ambulance
could be heard in the distance.

Isadore and Augusta finally emerged from the house followed
by Arthur, whose clenched jaws clearly expressed his
annoyance. Despite what she had just been through, Marilyn
was relaxed and dreamy-eyed, posing with her future in-laws
and snuggling up to Arthur, who forgot to light a cigarette
dangling from his mouth. Reporters were disappointed that he
refused to divulge the date of their wedding before ending the
press conference that lasted less than an hour.

According to Marilyn, it was Arthur's idea to slip over the
state line to White Plains, New York, and get married that night
by a municipal judge. Wearing a suit with no tie, the groom
borrowed his mother's wedding band for the brief civil
ceremony. Miller was so anxious to get married without fanfare
and publicity that his rushed bride wore a simple sweater and
skirt.

Two days later on Sunday, July 1, however, Marilyn was

resplendent in a champagne chiffon dress and matching veil. Carrying a bouquet of orchids, she and Arthur were secretly married again, this time at the nearby home of his agent, Kay Brown. They were wed in the Jewish faith by Rabbi Goldberg and exchanged Cartier wedding bands.

Twenty-five guests, including members of the Miller family, the Greenes and the Strasbergs, were invited to a wedding supper served in the garden. Arthur's sister said, "Marilyn was radiant. She was a vision. Her whole body glowed from within." On the back of a wedding portrait Marilyn wrote, "Hope, Hope, Hope."

On July 13, the newlyweds granted a brief interview at the airport before departing for England. Marilyn spoke about looking forward to working with Sir Laurence Olivier. Arthur was tired and most likely disturbed about traveling with an entourage and dealing with twenty-seven pieces of luggage. (Three belonged to him.) Supposedly Miller complained about lack of privacy and "living in a goldfish bowl." (He later denied this quote.) That his mood was somewhat gloomy could have been attributed to travelling with the Greenes and Strasbergs, whose influence over Marilyn was beginning to grate on his nerves. Reporters hinted all along that Miller was obviously trying to control his temper. They knew the playwright was a private person who avoided crowds and publicity. But he had been unable to resist Marilyn whom he described as "the most womanly woman I can imagine. She's kind of a lodestone that draws out of the male animal his essential qualities."

Marilyn's arrival in London was chaos. Reporters trampled one another in the mad rush and many photographers could not salvage their crushed cameras. Marilyn was terrified and Miller was outraged. Waiting to greet them at the airport was Sir Laurence and Lady Olivier (Vivien Leigh) who were both jostled, pushed and shoved. It was a relief for all concerned to get into their limousines.

The London *Evening News* cheered, "She is here. She walks. She talks. She really is as luscious as strawberries and cream."

The Millers rented Lord Moore's country mansion, Parkside House. It was surrounded by ten acres of well-manicured lawns and shrubs, and a stone wall. Olivier asked Marilyn if she was pleased with the accommodations. "Gosh," she replied, "you mentioned something about a cottage!"

"In England," he explained, "a home in the country is referred to as a cottage, my dear."

Olivier had scheduled a press conference at the Savoy Hotel for the following day. "Marilyn, dear," he pleaded, "please, pretty please we cannot be late tomorrow, we cannot. The press will take it very unkindly and half of them will be expecting it, so do me a favor and disappoint them, please."

Marilyn was an hour late. Sir Laurence was embarrassed but admitted she had the press eating out of her hand in no time. "The way she handled this difficult situation was an object lesson in charm," he said.

Olivier had done his research on Marilyn by seeking the advice of her former directors Josh Logan and Billy Wilder, who agreed that working with her was hell but worth all the trouble. Logan said, "Load up the camera and put Marilyn in front of it, and keep Paula Strasberg away from the set."

It was both a shock and disappointment to Olivier when he saw Paula at the airport because he saw no need for an acting coach. However, he tried to make the best of a touchy situation by going over the script with Paula. "Make Marilyn think it was her idea," she suggested. "You know what I mean?"

But Olivier found out soon enough that he was not dealing with an acting coach. Sitting in the front seat of a limo en route to the studio, he overheard Paula talking to Marilyn in the backseat: "My dear, you really must recognize your own potential. You haven't even yet any idea of the importance of your position in the world. You are the greatest sex symbol in human memory. Everybody knows and recognizes that, and you should too. It's a duty which you owe to yourself and to the world. It's ungrateful not to accept it. You are the greatest woman of your time, the greatest human being of your time; of any time, you name it. You can't think of anybody, I mean—no, not even Jesus—except you're more popular."

During the nauseating buttering up, Olivier was convinced that Paula was a nothing—not a teacher or advisor. Her only talent was praising Marilyn to reap the financial benefits for the Strasbergs.

Olivier also referred to Marilyn as "a schizoid," and the two people that she was could hardly have been more different. He was disillusioned before filming of *The Prince and the Showgirl* began when Marilyn came to rehearsals looking haggard and unkempt. "Bad skin with no makeup," he wrote in his memoirs.

Perhaps Olivier was disappointed in the woman with whom he had almost fallen in love, but at this stage his only concern was getting through the film and salvaging some degree of sanity. Despite his marriage falling apart after sixteen years, Vivien was pregnant, but miscarried on August 13. A close friend said, "I was more worried about Larry [Olivier] because Vivien was a manic depressive and he had been through hell with her. Now he had to deal with another mentally unbalanced woman, Marilyn Monroe, but maybe his experience with Vivien gave him a better insight into Marilyn, who did not have the training and concentration that Vivien did. Nor the professionalism, and this almost drove Larry off the edge. Because Marilyn owned the film and he was working for her, Larry had to stoop to the depths of humiliation though he covered it up very well."

Two weeks into filming, Miller flew home to visit his ailing daughter. Marilyn fell apart in his absence and did not report for work until he rushed back to London. Her "stomach problems" suddenly vanished, and filming resumed.

As a director, Olivier found it almost impossible to communicate with Marilyn. They were from two different schools of acting, but in striving to compromise, he was faced with Paula's prompting Marilyn, "Honey, just think of Coca-Cola and Frankie Sinatra!"

It took two days and over thirty-four takes for Marilyn to say just four words, "Oh, you poor prince." According to Olivier her dilemma was how to emphasize the word "poor" while nibbling and reacting to her first bite of caviar. Marilyn conferred with him and then with Paula over and over again. Finally he said, "Sit down, Marilyn, count to three and then say your line." She reacted with a blank stare. Olivier blurted out, "Can't you count, either?"

Trying the all-American approach, he told her to "look sexy." Marilyn retorted, "I *am* sexy!"

Observers disagree as to who was more to blame for the tension, Olivier or Monroe. But the facts speak for themselves, and Marilyn's tardiness and her lack of respect for those who went out of their way to make her comfortable and relaxed, in England and on the movie set, were very frustrating drawbacks.

It has since been established, however, that Marilyn came close to a nervous breakdown when she read Miller's diary, which he had left out. He referred to her as a troublesome bitch who wanted to be waited on night and day. What a waste of love!

When Marilyn read this, Arthur was in New York again with his ailing daughter who was referred to in the diary as the only one he truly loved. In a rare interview with author Fred Lawrence Guiles, Miller said he thought there was a misunderstanding because the lines quoted were from his new play *After the Fall*. In his diary, he said, there were references to his inability to help Marilyn and he was, as a result, of little use to her or to himself.

Marilyn's breakdown was kept quiet. Miller hurried back to England once again and summoned his wife's New York analyst, Marianne Kris. The press noted that the Queen's gynecologist paid a visit to Parkside House, and false rumors spread that Marilyn was pregnant. She had a history of menstrual cramps that were so painful, she was in agony for days. Her illness eased the tension with Arthur, and she was able to resume work.

Though Dr. Kris has been given credit for the positive change in Marilyn, observers felt that Paula's absence made all the difference in her behavior. It was Olivier who convinced Greene that it was best for all concerned if Paula left England.

Olivier's Russian friend, Irina Baranova, was on the set occasionally and remarked, "Marilyn loves to show herself, loves to be a star and the success that goes with it. But to be an actress is something she does not want at all. They were wrong to try to make one of her. She has wit, adorable charm, sex appeal and a bewitching personality. They are all part of her, not necessarily to be associated with any art or talent."

Olivier said Baranova discreetly captured his own feelings.

Marilyn and Arthur were not socially active in London, but they were obligated to accept invitations such as the one to meet Queen Elizabeth II at a reception following the Royal Film Performance. Though Arthur and the Oliviers were furious about having to wait for Marilyn, they were more concerned over what type of gown would cover those famous curves. She wore gold lamé, but the material draped beautifully over her body. Marilyn was confused when the Queen said, "How do you like your home? We're neighbors, you know."

"I'm not sure I understand. Don't you live at Buckingham Palace?"

"But we often live at Windsor Castle, so that makes us neighbors, doesn't it?"

"Oh, yes. Windsor Park! My husband and I have permits to ride our bicycles in *your* park."

Marilyn did, however, curtsy beautifully without revealing too much cleavage.

She made up for that at the London premiere of Miller's play, *A View from the Bridge*. The Oliviers, proper in manner and dress, went along to prove that they were all jolly good friends, publicity to the contrary.

Marilyn wore a very tight Jezebel-red dress that was cut so low, few eyes were on anything other than her breasts. Miller's play was acclaimed, but who cared? It was clearly Marilyn's night and when newsmen recovered, they criticized her for being cheap and making a public display of herself rather than "tone it down" for Miller's sake. Marilyn retorted, "Red is my husband's favorite color!" As for Arthur, he stuck up for her glorious femininity that proved to one and all what she was—Woman.

The British press reversed their opinion of Marilyn Monroe long before this incident. She had been aloof and short-tempered. Her tardiness and curt remarks on the movie set were not a secret. She browsed around London in wrinkled old clothes unbefitting a movie queen and proving how little she cared what anyone thought. The English were accustomed to seeing Hollywood celebrities, but these idols were always well-groomed and pleasant on the street.

Miller was distant and made it *very* clear from the beginning that he wanted privacy. At his best, however, he was not an outgoing, smiling and dynamic guy. Unlike Marilyn, his talent was contained in his writing, not in his being.

But the playwright and his wife were not in England to win a popularity contest. She was making a film with one of the most celebrated actors of our time. This, alone, afforded Marilyn favorable worldwide publicity that was sure to tempt the public.

The Prince and the Showgirl, the story of a Ruritanian prince, in London for the 1911 coronation, and a chorus girl with whom he had nothing in common, might never have reached the movie theaters if it hadn't been for Milton Greene, who somehow managed to work effectively with everyone concerned. But his business dealings on behalf of Marilyn Monroe Productions were met with opposition. Greene claimed he kept Marilyn informed, but—as a result of pill popping and steady drinking—she was in no condition to comprehend. Miller intervened before Greene made any firm commitments, and Marilyn sided with Arthur, who had read over her contractual agreement with Milton and was appalled by it. At the appropriate time, he told her, "Greene has to go."

Before leaving England, Marilyn came forth with an apology to the production staff. She had been a monster, but blamed it on ill health during most of the filming. With moist eyes, she asked everyone not to hold it against her.

On November 20, the Millers left England and a British newspaper wrote that Marilyn's exciting visit ended on a note "like the thud of a soggy crumpet." The Oliviers kept up appearances and were at the airport to embrace, kiss and bid farewell. The press hailed it as an absurd show: "Who do they think they're kidding?"

The Prince and the Showgirl was not a favorite of Monroe fans, and critics found it tedious. Bosley Crowther of the *New York Times* wrote, "The mere thought of Britain's great Shakespearean playing a romantic lead opposite Hollywood's most famous and least pedantic blonde is sufficient to start the mind imagining some highly comic scenes. And the mere sight of them is rewarding—for a while. . . . Miss Monroe mainly has to giggle, wiggle, breathe deeply and flirt. She does not make the showgirl a person, another of her pretty oddities ... both characters are essentially dull."

The *New York World-Telegram and Sun* thought Marilyn's acting promise had soared to a triumphant peak: "Laurence Olivier brings out qualities none of her [other] films ever summoned."

The *New York Herald-Tribune* wrote, "... Miss Monroe goes through the motions with mirth, squeals of pleasure and many a delightful toss of her rounded surfaces."

The usual wit contained in reviews of Marilyn's films failed to appear in those about *The Prince and the Showgirl*. Watching it today there remains, in the back of one's mind, a wonderment

Marilyn was married to her first husband, James Dougherty, from 1944 to 1946. *(UPI/Bettmann)*

Joseph Schenck, founder of 20th-Century Fox, was an old man, but Marilyn made him feel young again. *(UPI/Bettmann)*

Newlyweds Mr. and Mrs. DiMaggio leave San Francisco
City Hall on January 14, 1954.
(UPI/Bettmann Newsphotos)

A shattered
Marilyn faces
sympathetic
newsmen alone
after she and
DiMaggio separate.
*(UPI/Bettmann
Newsphotos)*

Screenwriter Robert Slatzer claims that he married
Marilyn in 1952. According to Slatzer, three days later,
her boss, Darryl Zanuck, demanded an annulment, but
Slatzer and Marilyn remained friends until her death.
(Courtesy of the Robert Slatzer Collection)

Robert Slatzer at
his exhibition of
his exclusive
photographs of
Marilyn taken on
the set of
*Something's Got to
Give*. *(Courtesy of
the Robert Slatzer
Collection)*

Marilyn with playwright Arthur Miller, whom she married in June 1956. They were divorced four years later. *(The Bettmann Archive)*

Marilyn with Yves Montand, her co-star in *Let's Make Love*. . . and they did, on and off the set. *(UPI/Bettmann)*

Marilyn arrives at New York's Idlewild Airport with Milton Greene, her lover and business partner in Monroe Productions. *(UPI/Bettmann)*

Marilyn's attention seems to wander as she dances with novelist Truman Capote at El Morocco. *(UPI/Bettmann)*

Marilyn Monroe and Montgomery Clift arrive at Loew's Capitol Theater for their preview of *The Misfits*. *(The Bettmann Archive)*

"I got goosebumps when Clark Gable touched me,"
Marilyn said about her famous leading man in *The Misfits*.
(AP/Wide World Photos)

Marilyn's fragile mental health would not survive her tumultuous affairs with both President John F. Kennedy and his brother, Attorney General Robert F. Kennedy. Her death on August 5, 1962 remains a mystery. *(UPI/Bettmann)*

The eternal movie star, a glamorous Marilyn Monroe
flashes a dazzling smile for her adoring fans.
(UPI/Bettmann)

that Monroe and Olivier would ever co-star in a film. He belonged on his side of the screen and she on the other. At the end, the prince and the showgirl go their separate ways. Another disappointment, but a logical one.

Twenty years after Olivier went through hell making *The Prince and the Showgirl*, he attended a dinner party. As a joke, the hostess ran the movie later that evening. "At the finish," he said, "everyone was clamorous in their praises. I was as good as could be, and Marilyn! Marilyn was quite wonderful, the best of all. So. What do you know?"

14

Pa

Marilyn's marriage to Arthur Miller had gotten off to a hectic start and suffered a setback in England, but they came home closer than ever. "We plan to grow old together," she said. Marilyn wanted to have a family and concentrate on being a housewife for a while. She called Arthur "Pa" or "Poppy" and, most assuredly, he fit her conception of the father image.

Until Marilyn began seeing a psychiatrist on a regular basis, she was not aware of her subconscious search for a man to take her father's place. Several Monroe historians claim that she was positive C. Stanley Gifford was her real father and that he refused to see or talk to Marilyn in later years.

Bob Slatzer denies this: "Edward Mortenson was listed as her father on the birth certificate. He disappeared shortly after Gladys became pregnant and she began dating other men including Gifford. It wasn't until Mortenson's death in 1929 that his marriage to Gladys officially ended.

"Marilyn asked me to locate Mortenson's death certificate since he was killed in a motorcyle accident in my home state of Ohio. It was filed under his real name Martin Edward Mortenson. The reason early biographers were never able to find proof of his death was that they did not know his first name."

Was it true that Marilyn tried to see Gifford?

Slatzer says, "Yes. She wanted to find out more about Mortenson, but Gifford was embarrassed about the publicity he had received. Marilyn was not illegitimate. She was born in wedlock, of Martin Edward Mortenson and Gladys Pearl Monroe Mortenson. These are the simple facts."

Perhaps Marilyn wanted to believe Gifford was her real father because she hinted as much. In a 1962 interview, she said, "My mother loved my father very much, but he wouldn't marry her. I don't think she ever recovered." Marilyn told her maid Lena Pepitone about getting in her mother's way: "A divorced woman [referring to John Baker] has enough problems, but one with an illegitimate baby. . . . "

Then there was the fantasy of incest which was Marilyn's way of getting revenge. Disguised in a black wig, she meets and seduces her father, then: "How do you feel now to have a daughter that you've made love to?"

She called her first husband Jim Dougherty "Daddy" and Joe DiMaggio's letters to her were signed "Pa."

Marilyn's longest and happiest marriage was to Arthur Miller, who was her knight in shining armor, her teacher, her lover and her confidant. Maybe, just maybe, he could have lived with that, but as her father, too, his creativity and concentration were diminished in the wasted hours that were spent pampering and caring for his famous wife.

Miller has been criticized for his lack of sympathy and understanding, but he was (and is) a great playwright who required time alone. Like most writers, Arthur had to take advantage of those days when ideas flowed easily on to the printed page and he did not want anyone, including Marilyn, to interrupt his creativity. Either she did not understand his needs or she resented Arthur's total concentration on anything other than her.

Hoping to do some writing in England, Miller was too busy getting Marilyn out of her stupor from sleeping pills and in shape to face the camera every day. Knowing she was extremely tense working with Olivier, he often stayed on the set.

Arthur did not expect Marilyn's desperate craving for attention and drugs to dominate his life. And, above all, he did not want to be an obligated father to the woman he loved. But Arthur's paternal sacrifices went beyond that of most devoted fathers until he finally bowed out to save himself.

When he returned to New York, Miller's first order of business was dissolving Marilyn's partnership with Milton Greene, who called it quits for $100,000. Arthur had read the fine print in the original agreement and explained the unprofitable facts to his wife.

Marilyn was hurt that Greene took advantage of her. She told Bob Slatzer, "I had a lot to drink, and in my hazy mind, signed the papers. I found out later that I had to share my one hundred thousand dollar salary with Milton, who was getting a straight salary of seventy-five thousand dollars. The company would lose money unless I did two or three pictures a year and I didn't want to do that."

Marilyn planned to continue her close business relationship with the Strasbergs, however. Miller was not pleased about this, but getting out of the city would distance him from them temporarily. He sold his "farmhouse" and bought a similar one that was badly in need of repairs. It was Marilyn's money that paid for their "new" place near Roxbury, but she was happier not living in the same house that Arthur shared with his first wife.

While their Connecticut hideaway was being renovated, the Millers rented a rundown cottage in Amagansett, Long Island, where Arthur was finally able to write without interruption.

In June of 1957, Marilyn became pregnant and she revelled in it, concentrating solely on being a housewife and serving Arthur's needs. She fussed over his children Bobby (nine) and Jane (twelve). They responded warmly, but had no conception of Marilyn Monroe's image and were more interested in the goodies they received on weekly visits to dear ol' dad.

Marilyn adored other people's children, but told Bob Slatzer she never wanted one of her own. "I don't think the insanity genes in Marilyn's family had anything to do with it," he said. "Like most actresses under contract to a studio, she was advised not to have babies because it would ruin her figure. But Marilyn was very happy with Miller and she thought the marriage would last forever. Knowing her as well as I did, Marilyn desperately wanted his child and to show him and, maybe herself, that she was a complete woman."

The Millers spent lazy days in the sun, walking along the beach and genuinely in accord. Marilyn enjoyed cooking for her husband and in-laws. She was particularly fond of Isadore, who was overwhelmed by her affection and sometimes a bit embarrassed, but he was a perceptive man who understood Marilyn's need for paternal love. She was close to Isadore until his death, which occurred after her divorce from Arthur.

It was in this contented and cheerful setting that Marilyn luxuriated in wearing old clothes, planning Miller's early breakfast and cooking a generous steak for dinner. One of her favorite hobbies at the old cottage on Long Island was tending her flowers. But on August 1, she screamed out in pain from the garden. Miller called an ambulance and she was rushed to Doctor's Hospital in Manhattan where her personal gynecologist determined that Marilyn had a tubular pregnancy. To prevent rupturing, she had to undergo surgery for the removal of a male embryo.

It was a blow to Marilyn for obvious reasons, but the good news was that she could have more children. The bad news was her inability to give up pills and booze, and her history of numerous abortions.

Marilyn told reporters she wanted to have lots of children and was adding a nursery to "Arthur's farm" in Roxbury. Her outlook was positive and she appeared to be recovering nicely. Because of her sensitivity, friends were amazed that Marilyn bounced back so quickly. But shortly after she was released from the hospital, Miller found her near death from an overdose of sleeping pills. The same thing happened once again and only Arthur's alertness saved her life.

In all fairness to Marilyn, these episodes might not have been suicide attempts. She was in the habit of taking too many pills, forgetting when and how many. Combined with champagne and other stimulants, she was oblivious and careless. During Marilyn's deliberate attempt to kill herself after Johnny Hyde's death, Natasha Lytess found a handful of pills dissolving in Marilyn's mouth. There was no doubt as to her motive. Seven years later Marilyn found happiness with Miller and had no reason to deliberately take an overdose of pills.

The very tragic aspect is that Marilyn felt so ambivalent about her own life that she was somewhat disappointed to wake up and face tomorrow because she had yet to fathom yesterday and all the yesterdays in the drug-induced haze of her life. If she was that close to death, so be it.

But Marilyn had "Pa," who resembled her father-hero Abraham Lincoln. A picture of the sixteenth president of the United States was in her bedroom. Miller and Lincoln were saviors, she said. They were men of integrity, respected for their brilliant minds and accomplishments. Arthur came into her life when she needed someone strong, but in 1957 Marilyn didn't know if her life was worth saving. Waking up from her self-induced comas, she melted in Arthur's arms, purring like a lost kitten. These tender moments were becoming few and far between, which leads one to believe Marilyn thought her near-death might bring them closer together.

Arthur was writing *The Misfits* with Marilyn in mind, and she loved the way her character was based on his observations. Marilyn was terrified of death (another reason to doubt the suicide theory), but this fear went beyond the human element. Miller watched her throw dead fish back into the sea, push stems of cut flowers in the earth and become hysterical over a wild animal lying dead by the roadside. (As Roslyn in the movie version of *The Misfits*, she fought to save wild mustangs.)

Marilyn was deeply touched that Arthur chose to focus on her vulnerability as a compassionate person. He understood her fragility and was willing to cope with it, she surmised.

Movie scripts arrived at 444 East 57th Street in New York every day. Marilyn's secretary or Miller looked them over and picked out the ones they thought might interest her, but the dialogue was scanned and the pages strewn on the floor. The months dragged on, Miller busy in his room with the door closed and Marilyn dozing, drinking or visiting her psychiatrist.

Arthur finally read a proposal for a film called *Some Like It Hot*. Marilyn liked the part of the singer in an all-girl band during Prohibition. She was thrilled that Billy Wilder (*The Seven Year Itch*) was directing and very excited over the possibility of working with Frank Sinatra. But when Marilyn read the entire script, she was furious. "Another dumb blonde!" she wailed. "Too dumb to recognize a couple of guys in drag!" The worst blow was finding out that Sinatra was unavailable.

"I don't want to do it," she told Miller. "I don't and I won't!"

He thought it was a very good script, but she fought him bitterly and would not change her mind. In reflection, Arthur was right about *Some Like It Hot*, but trying to convince his wife resulted in her ranting and raving for days. She was overheard yelling at him, "Is that all you think I am? Just another dumb blonde?" Miller emphasized her great timing as a comedienne and how much the public loved *The Seven Year Itch*. Marilyn retorted, "That was believable, but not this Sugar Kane who is so dumb she can't tell a man from a woman!"

Miller eventually got through to her when they were offered a percentage of the gross instead of the usual flat fee. At first Marilyn balked at making money: "Who needs it?"

Arthur replied, "We do."

Almost two years had passed since Marilyn's last film *The Prince and the Showgirl*. She paid off Milton Greene, spent untold sums of money on "Arthur's farm" in Roxbury, and supported a staff of three or four at her Manhattan apartment, not to mention Paula's coaching fees. Though the Millers rarely entertained, Marilyn was accustomed to drinking Piper-Heidsieck all day, every day.

The Millers were far from broke, however. Arthur thought *Some Like It Hot* was a golden opportunity, but his main concern was Marilyn's persistent depression brought about by the loss of their baby. He thought her going back to work was the best and, maybe, the only answer. Marilyn gave in reluctantly, but was sorry she did when news reached her that the movie was going to be filmed in black-and-white.

Wilder explained to Marilyn that Curtis and Lemmon, made up as females, looked offensive in color and the censors might object. Even though the men were running from gangsters after witnessing the St. Valentine's Day massacre and forced to dress up like women or get killed, this was a very touchy subject. Marilyn gave in after viewing color tests of Curtis and Lemmon, but insisted she would never make another black and white film again.

Disgusted with the whole project, Marilyn put on twenty pounds in defiance. The only person who could reason with her was Paula Strasberg, who thought the part of Sugar Kane had wonderful possibilities and she emphasized Marilyn's three numbers, "I Wanna Be Loved by You," "Runnin' Wild," and "I'm Through with Love." Paula's presence in Hollywood was the most assuring aspect for Marilyn.

Arthur had finished *The Misfits* and planned to discuss his screenplay with Clark Gable in California. "I've never been able to connect stars with parts I write," Miller said, "but after meeting Gable I could see him as Gay Langland. It was his secret charm—tough but responsive to feeling and ideals." Even though Marilyn would be in the film with the great John Huston directing, Gable wavered: "Gay Langland has a truck and a dog and that's all." He didn't understand Gay Langland, but Miller said, "You're just like him!" Gable agreed to do *The Misfits*, but waited to sign a contract until he was offered more money than anyone else in Hollywood had ever gotten.

When *Some Like It Hot* was finished, Billy Wilder thought he deserved a Purple Heart because he was the only director who had worked with Marilyn Monroe on two films. "I can now look at my wife without wanting to hit her because she's a woman," he said.

Marilyn's tardiness wore him out, as it did Tony Curtis and Jack Lemmon. Once she arrived to find the set was closed down for the day. When she showed up—always late—Wilder was exasperated by the number of retakes. He counted over fifty because Marilyn could not remember three words.

Tony Curtis, who was at his best in one or two takes, took a beating. While Marilyn rose to her peak, he was winding down and listless. As filming progressed, Curtis became extremely annoyed with her and she sensed this, but it came to light when they were watching the rushes of the two making love. Someone asked Tony how it felt to kiss Marilyn Monroe and he replied, "It's like kissing Hitler." A technician didn't think that was a very nice thing to say. "Really?" Curtis scowled. "You try acting with her!"

In November 1958, Miller told Wilder, "Marilyn's pregnant. Would you go easy on her?"

"If she shows up on time, I'll let her go home early," the director replied.

Marilyn was so elated, however, she had no intention of getting up early and rushing to the set. "I have to think of my baby," she said.

Everyone involved with *Some Like It Hot* was relieved when the film was finished in November. Jack Lemmon said little about Marilyn other than he was hot and miserable wearing heavy makeup, wigs and padding under his clothes while he waited hours for her. Then he had to endure endless retakes in high heels.

Billy Wilder's nerves were shattered. As for working with
Marilyn again he said in an interview, "My doctor and my
psychiatrist say I'm too old and too rich to go through that
again."

Marilyn returned to New York and stayed in bed. She was
determined to rest until the birth of her baby, but on December
17, 1958, suffered a miscarriage. She put the blame on Arthur
for making her do *Some Like It Hot*. The fact that their marriage
was strained was apparent to close friends. She attended classes
at the Actors Studio while he concentrated on his writing
behind closed doors. The few guests who came to their
apartment on the thirteenth floor at 444 East 57th Street claim
they saw Arthur only when he walked his dog. The best he
could offer was a polite "Hello." The situation was not much
different in Roxbury, so Marilyn's visits to the country ceased.

Wilder's stinging comments about her made the newspapers,
and she cursed at Miller viciously. The servants heard Marilyn
shouting, "Do something! People listen to you because they
respect you! It's your fault, anyway. They made me look like a
fat freak!"

Arthur contacted Wilder and demanded a retraction. The
director replied, "I hereby acknowledge that good wife Marilyn
is a unique personality. . . . but in the words of Joe E. Brown,
'Nobody's perfect.' " This was a quote from *Some Like It Hot*.
At the end of the film, Joe E. Brown proposes marriage to
Daphne (Lemmon), who confesses he's really a man. Brown
smiles broadly and says, "Nobody's perfect."

There are conflicting stories as to Marilyn's relationship with
Wilder and Curtis. She looked forward to working with her
favorite director and thought Tony was very sexy. During their
prolonged kissing scene, Marilyn was overzealous, parting her
lips to devour his mouth. Who started the rumors that she was
indeed French-kissing isn't known, but she never denied it.

Onlookers suspect she was either enamoured of Curtis or trying to make Miller jealous.

As for Wilder, it's been established that she disliked him when they were working together, but at a party before the film was completed, Marilyn spent the evening flirting with him. It's doubtful she was trying to seduce the director, but this proves how nervous, temperamental and demanding she was facing the camera. It also proves that Marilyn believed she could win any battle in the bedroom, where, unfortunately, Miller did not spend much time. When he did, she did not change the sheets and remained in bed all day reminiscing.

The New York premiere of *Some Like It Hot* was at Loew's State on March 30, 1959. Marilyn had not planned to attend, but at the last minute changed her mind. Still overweight, she squeezed into a silver lamé gown and waved to throngs of fans, Miller at her side. This was the best part of the evening for Marilyn, who covered her face when she appeared on the screen. The audience, including Arthur, howled uproariously. She concluded they were laughing at her, even when she got a standing ovation at the end. In tears, Marilyn ran up the aisle, out of the theater and into her limousine, with Arthur trying not to be left behind.

When they got home, she told him, "It was disgusting! I was a fat pig! Did you hear them laugh at me?"

Arthur said it was a great movie. Very funny.

She grabbed another bottle of champagne and screamed, "Shut up! I was a funny fat whore! That's why they laughed!" With that she slammed her bedroom door and locked it.

Marilyn seldom, if ever, mentioned *Some Like It Hot* again. She never got over the ugly experience despite smashing reviews. The movie made millions, but she did not live long enough to reap the harvest. If she had, money could not have erased the bitter memories. Marilyn complained about her weight, but she was just as zaftig in *The Seven Year Itch* and just as pregnant. Her gowns in *Some Like It Hot* left very little to the imagination, however. They were sheer, cut low in the front and back, with her breasts overflowing. What she saw at the premiere was what she saw every night in the screening room so it came as no surprise.

Her involvement with the Actors Studio put Marilyn in a state of limbo. Her closest friends blame New York for what happened to the bouncy blonde who once said the only thing she had on when she went to bed was the radio.

She wanted to improve herself and earn respect from her peers, but in the process got caught up in the theater web of professionals. She talked about doing a Broadway show because, "I hate Hollywood. There are lots of blondes with big tits out there. Everybody kisses everybody and it doesn't mean shit." But Marilyn failed to understand that she was blessed with a magic only the screen could define and that the movie camera was her loyal and devoted friend who made even the likes of Sir Laurence Olivier envious.

Billy Wilder said the Strasbergs had given Marilyn more acting depth, but her real talent came naturally. Having a coach on the set hindered her from letting go and using her instinct—an inborn quality so many fine actors did not possess. Trying to be someone else was a losing battle—as was her marriage to a dedicated writer. And no one was more aware of this than Miller, who wanted Marilyn as she was when he found her. Proof of this was *Some Like It Hot*.

The *New York Post*'s Archer Winsten wrote, 'Marilyn does herself proud, giving a performance of such intrinsic quality that you begin to believe she's only being herself and it is herself who fits into that distant period and this picture so well."

A.H. Weiler in the *New York Times* said the movie was outrageously funny: "… As the band's somewhat simple singer ukulele-player, Miss Monroe, whose figure simply cannot be overlooked, contributes more assets than the obvious ones to this madcap romp. She sings a couple of whispery old numbers and also proves to be the epitome of a dumb blonde and a talented comedienne."

Jack Lemmon was the only member of the cast nominated for an Oscar, but he lost to Charlton Heston in *Ben-Hur*.

Marilyn was not entirely left out, however. She was thrilled to receive two foreign awards for *The Prince and the Showgirl* in 1958. Italy gave her the David di Donatello prize and the French Film Institute presented Marilyn with the Crystal Star.

Arthur Miller was chosen by the National Institute of Arts and Letters for the Gold Medal in Drama. He accepted this prestigious honor (bestowed every five years) with mixed emotions. He had accomplished nothing during his marriage to Marilyn, who consumed his time and drained his concentration. What troubled him most was knowing she was unaware of this—an innocent little girl who thought Daddy could make the pain go away.

15

Yves

To the Europeans and Asians, America was Coca-Cola and
Marilyn Monroe. Even behind the Iron Curtain of the Soviet
Union she had an admirer in Premier Nikita Khrushchev who
was touring the United States in September 1959. Twentieth
Century-Fox invited him to a studio luncheon on the set of
Can-Can, with Frank Sinatra and Shirley MacLaine. It was a
star-studded event, and Marilyn wanted very much to be there.
Miller, who had yet to satisfy the House Un-American
Activities Committee as to his political affiliations, felt it best if
he stayed in New York.

Krushchev took Marilyn's hand and squeezed it. "You're a
very pretty girl," he said.

"My husband, Arthur Miller, sends you his greetings." She
smiled. "There should be more of this type of thing. It would
help both our countries understand each other."

In an interview, Marilyn said, "It was an historic moment."
But she told her friends that the leader of the U.S.S.R. had too
many warts on his face. "Who would want to be a Communist
with a president like that?" she exclaimed. Nonetheless,
Marilyn thought he was infatuated with her. "I could tell he
liked me best of all," she said.

Back in 1956, Achmed Sukarno, President of Indonesia, took

a shine to her at a Beverly Hills party. Marilyn responded, to the delight of the other guests who watched sensual sparks fly between the two. She confided in Bob Slatzer that Sukarno spent the night with her.

Anthony Summers wrote, in his well-researched book entitled *Goddess: The Secret Lives of Marilyn Monroe*, "Whatever happened at the original meeting, it had not gone unnoticed by the CIA. In those years Indonesia loomed as large as Vietnam." Summers goes on to say there were inside rumors that the CIA wanted to curry favor with Sukarno by using Marilyn as bait, but nothing came of it.

When 20th Century-Fox offered Elizabeth Taylor $1 million to do *Cleopatra*, Marilyn complained, "They're paying me a lousy one hundred thousand dollars!" Obligated to make three more films for Fox, she decided to get them over with so she could be independent and demand the price she was worth.

Fox offered Marilyn *Let's Make Love*, the story of a billionaire who puts up the money for a play and is mistaken for an auditioning actor. Marilyn's role was, as usual, a showgirl who wants nothing to do with wealthy men. She falls in love with the billionaire thinking he's broke. The ending is easy to figure out.

"It's not a great script," Marilyn said, "but if it means getting out of my Fox contract sooner, who cares?" She wanted Rock Hudson to co-star, but he turned it down, as did Cary Grant. Gregory Peck agreed and then backed out because he wasn't pleased with Mr. Miller's revisions that favored Mrs. Miller. There was also the problem of top billing. Marilyn expected it and Peck insisted on it. Had there been a compromise, *Let's Make Love* would have turned out much better than it did.

Marilyn, who had been in hospital for what the press described as "gynecological surgery of a corrective nature," was told by doctors that they were not optimistic about her chances of having a baby, but they did not rule it out, either. When she returned home and found out that a long list of Hollywood's best leading men had turned down the opportunity to co-star with her in *Let's Make Love*, she was deeply hurt. "What's wrong with me?" she asked Arthur. "I can't have a baby and I can't find anyone who wants to work with me." He told Marilyn not to panic because he was going to introduce her to an actor who was perfect for the part of the billionaire.

When Miller was in England, he flew to Paris to see the French film production of his play *The Crucible* and became acquainted with its stars Yves Montand and his actress wife Simone Signoret. Montand was a staunch socialist and, like Miller, had problems with his visas and passports. But in September 1959, Yves made it to Broadway in a one-man song-and-dance show that was acclaimed by critics, and held over for several weeks. This gave Miller the opportunity to invite the Montands for dinner to meet his wife.

Marilyn was attracted to Yves from the moment he walked in the door. She said he bore a striking resemblance to Joe DiMaggio and was more intrigued to find out that Montand was not, as most people supposed, French but Italian. He spoke very little English, but the bright and talented Simone translated for Marilyn. It was a gay evening, and Arthur contributed more to the conversation and festivities than he had in a long time.

After Marilyn saw Yves' show, she could talk about no one else. He came to her apartment several times to discuss *Let's Make Love*. Arthur was anxious for them to become acquainted, leaving them alone while he worked in his study.

Montand agreed to play the billionaire, but the studio and Paula Strasberg did not think he was right for the part. Marilyn used her influence and won. Miller said he was relieved to see his wife smile again and overjoyed that she was so happy about working for a change.

Yves Montand was born Ivo Livi in Monsummano, Italy, in 1921. His father was an Italian socialist forced to flee the country when Mussolini took over. The poverty-stricken family settled in France when Yves was two. He was forced to drop out of school at the age of eleven and worked as a laborer until he tried his luck at singing in Marseille nightclubs. In 1944 he met the great singer Edith Piaf, who nurtured his talents on the stage and in her bed. Yves was not, by far, the first or the last of Piaf's long string of lovers, but he was the only man to whom she was faithful. Yves, six years younger than Edith, wanted to marry her, but she was obsessed with making him a star. She succeeded three years later, but lost interest in Montand when he was able to fend for himself.

Simone Signoret wrote in her memoirs that Yves was deeply hurt when Piaf left him, for they had enjoyed good times together. "She had not taught him everything," Simone said, "for one already has within oneself the things that no one can teach anyone."

Montand remained primarily a singer until 1953, when he was featured in his first major film *Le Salaire de la Peur* (*The Wages of Fear*).

Yves married Simone in 1951 after her divorce from French director Yves Allegret with whom she had a daughter, Catherine. Of her marriage to Montand she said, "We have quarreled a lot, but that is good. Otherwise things would have been very sad." They remained together until her death in 1985.

Miss Signoret, who assumed her mother's maiden name, was born Simone Kaminker in Wiesbaden, Germany, in 1921. Her father, who was a linguist, escaped to England during World War II and joined the Free French. Simone supported her mother and sister in Paris by working as an English tutor and typist. Encouraged by a friend, she began as an extra in films and rose to fame quickly in 1946.

Simone appeared older than Yves because of her short stocky figure, composed manner and matronly facial features. But her brilliance as an actress brought out a rare beauty and magnetism.

Montand, in contrast, was tall and slim with dreamy eyes and a continental manner that came across on and off the screen.

He knew little about Marilyn Monroe and had never seen one of her movies. They met at a time when she had lost faith in her marriage and her ability to have a child. These factors made Marilyn sexually vulnerable.

In her fantasy, she had found another DiMaggio, whose picture hung in her closet. Montand was a close second, and she studied him very carefully. He was sweet, romantic, considerate and attentive, but unlike the Yankee Clipper, Yves was a performer who communicated with her about show business, despite his bad English.

Marilyn did not think the Montands were suited to one another: "Simone's too old for him. She's Arthur's type." But the two couples got along very well and spent a good deal of time together—a social rarity for the Millers.

In January of 1960, they checked into the Beverly Hills Hotel, bungalows 20 and 21. Marilyn and Yves went to the studio together every morning, leaving Arthur at work on *The Misfits*. Late afternoon he and Simone had cocktails while they waited for their spouses.

Marilyn actually enjoyed doing *Let's Make Love*. "I'm not nervous with Yves," she said. There were only a few huddles with Paula Strasberg, much to the relief of director George Cukor. Marilyn was late occasionally, and Montand politely, but firmly, told her to please let him know when she had a change of plans. If Yves was aware of her reputation for tardiness, he didn't say so other than "... capricious little girls have never amused me."

But Marilyn *had* to lean on someone, and that someone was Yves. He was unable to get a good grip on his role because of Marilyn's grip on him. As a result, Montand's performance was wooden, and George Cukor could do nothing about it.

Miller knew that Marilyn was attracted to Montand and, given the opportunity, would get what she wanted. Obviously Arthur didn't care since he went out of town so often. Was this a deliberate attempt to prompt a divorce? If so, was he prepared to do *The Misfits* without Marilyn? No one knows the answer to either question, but the gossips were speculating.

Simone remained at the Beverly Hills Hotel, but after winning an Oscar for Best Actress in *Room at the Top* that spring, she was deluged with film offers. Her leisure days were soon over and she had to fly to Europe. Arthur returned to Hollywood briefly and then decided he wanted to see his children in New York.

Montand found himself alone with Marilyn and wasn't sure how to handle it. He'd had more than his share of women, but getting involved with his leading lady in the middle of a picture was a touchy situation. How much Yves knew about Marilyn's instability isn't known. He sensed, however, that she wanted more than one night of lovemaking and, after that, she would be in control of him until the film was finished. If he balked, Marilyn could make his life sheer hell. Montand waited for her to make the first move and did not have to wait long. She knocked on his bungalow door wearing nothing but a mink coat. When she opened it, the affair began. "What else was I to do?" he said.

One of Marilyn's former lovers, journalist Jim Bacon, received a phone call from a waiter friend at the Beverly Hills Hotel who had served breakfast-in-bed to the lovers. Smelling a scoop, Bacon called the bungalow. Yves ranted in French and hung up. A few minutes later Marilyn's press agent called Bacon explaining that the stars were only going over their script together. Besides, they're just good friends. "We both knew it was a lot of horseshit," Bacon said.

Stories circulated around Hollywood like bees around honey. One of the best was Miller looking for his pipe in both bungalows and finding his wife in bed with Yves. There was also a titter over a rumor that Marilyn asked her husband to write a part for Montand in *The Misfits*.

As the romance progressed, the much-talked-about couple went to parties with a third person to make it appear casual.

Yves put on a good act, but Marilyn never left his side. They did not embarrass themselves by kissing or holding hands. This probably would have been accepted as part of the game, but no one could overlook Montand's ability at getting Marilyn to their destinations on time. If Hollywood insiders took pot shots at each other, they were staunch defenders of one another to the outside world, and to avoid the unusual attention that Marilyn got by arriving late, Yves was warned to make sure she came early. He said that was no problem because she would do anything he asked her to do. To the fascination of those who knew Marilyn, they were amazed when Yves wanted to go home and she lingered too long. He left without her and Marilyn was last seen running after his car.

Miller eventually came back to the Beverly Hills Hotel and wondered why he hadn't seen Montand who, in all good conscience, could not pretend things were the same. His trysts with Marilyn were at the studio or elsewhere. This put the burden of the affair entirely on her since it was she who had to face Miller in the evenings. Marilyn was reeling from the strain of discussing divorce with Arthur knowing that Yves had given her no reason whatsoever to assume he would marry her. Miller was concerned about the publicity if Marilyn announced their divorce before filming *The Misfits*, which was about to go into production. Arthur knew the marriage was beyond repair and that he was no longer Marilyn's savior because he had left her alone in Hollywood as he had when they were in England. She said he had betrayed her.

Howard Hughes was staying in a bungalow at the Beverly Hills Hotel and came to the same conclusion that everyone else did, according to pal Brian Evans, "If Miller was in love with Marilyn and sincere about saving the marriage, he should have been with her. Obviously, he wasn't," Brian related. "She was thrown to the wolves, if you'll excuse the pun. Howard hinted that Montand had lots of girls and some of them were well known in show business. Furthermore, he was in love with his wife, who was smarter and wiser than the whole bunch. She knew how to keep her man. Simone looked the other way when her husband had flings because he always came back, which is typical of European marriages."

Columnist Hedda Hopper talked to Montand about the affair privately. In broken English he said there was nothing serious between him and Marilyn, a sweet and simple girl, who misinterpreted his gestures of tenderness. "I thought Marilyn was as sophisticated as some of the other ladies I have known," Yves explained.

Hedda apparently misinterpreted him, too, because she wrote that Montand said Marilyn had a "schoolgirl crush" on him. He denied saying it and added, "Miss Hopper put words in my mouth that weren't there." Marilyn was very hurt, but she wanted to believe Yves' explanation that he was misquoted. Miller paid no attention, but Simone was worried that the publicity might backfire and hurt her husband's career. In later years she said people wrote letters urging her to "hold on" and "don't worry. He'll come back." The truth was, Simone said, "Yves had come home as planned and we were getting on with our lives. But the rumors refused to die. When reporters came to our home, he rattled in French until I explained that he was afraid they would ask about Marilyn Monroe. If she is in love with my husband, it proves she has good taste because I am in love with him, too."

Though Yves and Marilyn were not as discreet as they should have been, there are many people who blame him for using her and for exposing their affair in his interview with Hedda Hopper. We will never know what he promised Marilyn, but if Montand led her to believe their relationship was serious, he might have been considered a cad. "She's not well," he told a confidant. "Anyone can see she's on pills. I don't want the responsibility." Perhaps Yves did not know the extent of her emotional instability any more than Arthur Miller did when he married her.

*

Marilyn completed *Let's Make Love* in June of 1960 and returned to New York before starting *The Misfits*. She told Bob Slatzer that Montand needed her and she hoped they would marry. "He's flying to France in a few days," Marilyn said, "and changing planes at Idlewild. I'm going to be there and surprise him!" Under another name she reserved a room at a hotel near the airport, and with roses and champagne in the limousine, Marilyn popped out from behind a pillar in the terminal as he approached the lounge. Montand was dumbstruck when he saw her, and she was horrified that he was travelling with an entourage of press agents, reporters and studio personnel.

The airport was swarming with people due to a bomb scare and all flights were delayed for several hours. Yves agonized that the press would have a field day, and Marilyn was disappointed that her romantic interlude had turned into a mad scramble for privacy. It was decided that Montand would be more comfortable waiting for his flight at the nearby International Hotel. He and Marilyn were seen leaving the terminal in her limousine and together in the hotel lobby. James Bacon, who apparently had contacts in all the right places, got a call from an employee at the International, and it was assumed the lovers enjoyed a romantic interlude between planes. But Marilyn and Yves were not alone except for a brief conversation. He said their relationship had been wonderful, but he would never leave Simone. "Perhaps," he said, "you and Arthur will visit us in Paris." Yves kissed her, dashed from the limousine and boarded his plane for France.

It was a humiliating night for Marilyn. Montand made no effort to be alone with her at the hotel or throw a crumb of hope for another time, another place. He was clearly vexed that she had come to Idlewild. It was bad enough that he told her the blunt truth, but the press witnessed a rebuffed Marilyn, a clumsy situation that needed no explanation. Her gifts of champagne and caviar told the whole ugly story.

Once again, Marilyn felt unwanted and alone, as she had during a childhood that now might not have seemed so bleak after all, considering her present heartbreaks. In her plight to believe that the many sacrifices had been worth the tragic letdowns, Marilyn embellished on her pitiful beginnings in a desperate and subconscious attempt to convince herself that life was worth living.

Miller remained locked in his study with *The Misfits* while Marilyn brooded over making another black-and-white film. Gable signed for $750,000, 10 percent of the gross and, aware of Marilyn's habits of tardiness and absences, $48,000 a week for overtime. If he resented being called the King, Gable rejoiced in making the highest salary offered a star to do a motion picture. "The hell with a throne," he winked. "I'll take the dough."

Marilyn was upset over everything concerning *The Misfits*. She blamed Arthur for not insisting on color, for changing her dialogue and not demanding more money. (They were splitting half a million.) He accused her of being unprofessional and he could no longer deal with her behavior on the movie set. "My nerves are frayed, too," he said.

Lena Pepitone wrote in her memoirs that Marilyn banged on Miller's door screaming, "I'm your wife. It's not your movie, it's ours. Now you say it's yours. You lied!" When Miller didn't answer, she threw a champagne bottle against the mirror behind her bed. The sheets were covered with glass, and she kept slamming her body against the closet door. Pepitone said, "I grabbed her and held her tight so she wouldn't hurt herself. Mr. Miller did not sleep in the apartment that night or any other night before they left for Nevada to do *The Misfits*."

Pepitone recalled seeing *Let's Make Love* with Marilyn, who enjoyed her version of "My Heart Belongs to Daddy," but wept at the end of the movie when she married Montand.

The *New York World-Telegram and Sun* thought *Let's Make Love* was a "gay, preposterous and completely delightful romp." Bosley Crowther of the *New York Times* devoted most of his review to Milton Berle who, appearing as himself, tries to teach the billionaire how to tell a joke. "There is a heaviness in Montand," Crowther wrote. "His heavy French accent makes him hard to understand. His accent is a poor excuse for charm. The old Monroe dynamism is lacking in the things she is given to do. It doesn't seem very important that she is finally brought together with Mr. Montand."

16

Gable

Marilyn was relying on pills and liquor to cope with her never-ending personal problems. She took Nembutal to sleep, Benzedrine to wake up and a variety of tranquilizers. Though she continued to consult psychiatrist Marianne Kris in New York, Marilyn was seeing more of Dr. Ralph Greenson in Los Angeles, who had been recommended by Frank Sinatra. Greenson tried to save her marriage, but Arthur said he had done all he could. The doctor described Miller as having "the attitude of a father who had done more than most fathers would do." Ethics prevented Greenson from exposing the confidences of his patients, but he commented on what can be considered his observations. Until Marilyn's death, Greenson tried to wean her off sleeping pills, in particular, but she managed to sweet-talk other doctors into writing prescriptions. Greenson caught on to this in the last few months of Marilyn's life, but she cleverly got or "stole" sleeping pills from friends. Her heavy intake of uppers and downers began during *The Prince and the Showgirl* and leveled off when she was living at peace with Miller. But the Montand affair and working in *The Misfits* were dangerous setbacks for Marilyn, who had little to look forward to other than sleep and dulling the pain of living in the waking hours. She hated the 100 degree temperature in Nevada and sharing a hotel suite with Arthur.

John Huston, who had directed Marilyn in *The Asphalt Jungle* a decade before, was shocked to see his leading lady in a daze of dope. After a few days of filming *The Misfits*, he pleaded with Miller, "You've got to get Marilyn off those drugs." Huston didn't know about the pending divorce, of course. He told the doctor on location not to give Marilyn any pills, but she got a supply elsewhere. Huston thinks she went to a local doctor who gave Marilyn Monroe anything she wanted.

The Misfits revolved around a Reno divorcée (Marilyn) who meets three drifting cowboys (Clark Gable, Montgomery Clift and Eli Wallach) in Nevada rounding up mustangs for money from a dog-food factory. She saves the wild horses and lassoes Gable. The film is dreary, at best, and wallows in self-pity, but it bears the distinction of being the last movie made by Gable and Monroe. In the final scene he says to her, "Honey, we all got to go sometime, reason or no reason. Dyin's as natural as livin'. Man who's afraid to die is too afraid to live, far as I've ever seen. So, there's nothing to do but forget it, that's all. Seems to me." Many movie historians consider this the highlight of *The Misfits* other than watching the King steal every scene from his Method-acting co-stars. Gable grinned over their "getting into the part" and said, "I bring to it everything I have been, everything I am and everything I hope to be."

The cast admired him for it, but Marilyn was terrified of working with Gable. She arrived late, walked in his direction, but ran the other way to throw up. When she finally approached the King, Marilyn whispered, "I'm sorry for being late." He put his big arm around her and said softly, "You're not late, honey." Then he whispered something and she giggled.

Clark Gable was fifty-nine and a movie veteran of over thirty years. He had started out as an extra in films and never forgot the tough times even after he signed a contract with MGM. He was also a veteran of five marriages. His favorite wives were Carole Lombard, who died in a plane crash, and his current spouse, Kay Spreckels, who became pregnant with his first child during *The Misfits*.

Gable had shared his bed with hundreds of women, including Joan Crawford, Ava Gardner, Lana Turner, Loretta Young and Grace Kelly. Partial to blondes, the King would have slipped off with Marilyn for certain, but he was winding down. Doctors wouldn't insure him for the film unless he rested in bed for a week. Amphetamines and liquor might have been a factor. (Montgomery Clift couldn't pass the physical until he eased off booze and pills.)

Marilyn still carried the picture of Gable that her mother had passed off as "your father." She believed it to be true for a long time and her dream of incest might have been a reality had the King been a few years younger. Marilyn was not one to give up, however. Gable's stand-in Lew Smith said that *The Misfits* was a circus and the cast made up a pretty fair sideshow. "Miss Monroe was in there pitching," Smith said. "She wanted Clark and he was a big tease. He liked to pat her plump fanny, knowing she never wore anything underneath. Or he'd pinch her and whisper goodies in her ear. She asked him how he put up with the press and the fans and mobs of people. She hated it. Clark said when things got tough he took out his false teeth, and he actually took them out. 'Then I do my Gabby Hayes impersonation,' he said. Miss Monroe looked at him adoringly. Teeth or no teeth, she said he was the best thing that ever happened to her."

Smith said that Marilyn was too nervous to see reporters so Gable offered to take over. "I know I'm a poor substitute," he grinned, "but maybe it'll pacify them." And he defended her to the press: "She's a sensitive little girl. Besides, it's awfully hot here. Well over a hundred."

One scene in *The Misfits* gave Marilyn a chance to get closer to Gable. He walks into the bedroom and finds her wrapped only in a sheet. "I was so thrilled when he kissed me," she said. "We had to do the scene over several times. Then the sheet dropped and he put his hand on my breast. I got goose bumps all over. That night I didn't need a sleeping pill. I dreamed that we did it. God, I was in heaven. Whenever he's near me, I want him to kiss me, kiss me, kiss me. There were times I thought he was giving in—that he'd ask to meet me somewhere later. We did a lotta kissing, touching and feeling, and I never tried harder to seduce any man. His wife caught us snuggling. I don't think she likes me, but I don't care. She's got him. I don't."

Gable was frustrated over many things. Reno was a wild town, and everyone was having more fun than he was—picking up girls, gambling and staying up late until the bars closed. He wanted to go back in time, do some carousing, spend one wild night with Marilyn and wake up with blurred memories of empty liquor bottles and the blonde who went back to her own room.

Gable envied John Huston's wild binges and orgies. He resented the wild stories he heard in detail every morning. He had done all this with style a few years before, but didn't brag about it. Clark Gable didn't have to. "In my day," he said, "I used to take off on Fridays and show up Monday morning for work in my tux. That told the whole lovely story. . . . "

While Marilyn raved about the King, she ranted at Miller in front of everyone. Huston said he knew the marriage was over when Marilyn drove off in their car after work, leaving Arthur "alone in the desert." Then it became common knowledge that the Millers were sleeping in separate suites. Despite this arrangement, he often looked in on her to make sure she had not taken too many sleeping pills, but it happened, anyway. On August 26th, she overdosed. After her stomach was pumped, Marilyn was wrapped in a wet sheet, carried to a plane, and flown to the Westside Hospital in Los Angeles the next day. Doctors said she was suffering from exhaustion. Huston doubted that Marilyn would be able to finish *The Misfits*, but was optimistic after he and Miller saw her in the hospital.

Marilyn knew that Yves Montand was in town dubbing some

lines for *Let's Make Love*, but he did not return her calls. From an unknown source, she found out he would be in New York for Christmas and made up her mind to see him then.

Though Marlon Brando and Frank Sinatra came to the hospital, it was a visit from DiMaggio that perked her up. Before she returned to Reno, Marilyn stopped off in San Francisco to see Joe.

Meanwhile, Gable waited and waited and waited. He was anxious to finish the movie and go home. Bored and restless, he began drinking heavily in the 115-degree heat. Dressed in western garb with an open script on his lap, he smoked one cigarette after the other and drank whatever booze was available. He watched the men work with the wild horses, and was convinced he could do most of his own stunts. Surprisingly, no one tried to stop him, including Huston. While his stand-in and stuntman stayed helplessly on the sidelines, Gable balanced himself on the hood of a car, rolled across it, and fell to the pavement. In another scene he was dragged by a truck travelling twenty-five miles per hour. He wrestled with a wild stallion, got snarled in a lariat and was dragged face down until a wrangler could stop the horse.

Kay Gable knew nothing about this until one night she saw him coming out of the shower. "He was bruised and bloody on one side. When I asked him what happened he said he was dragged on a rope 'by accident.' I told him he was out of his mind."

Marilyn finally returned to Reno, and Gable greeted her with "Get to work, beautiful." Her tardiness continued, but he quipped, "Why are sexy women always late?" When she knew her lines, he kissed her on the lips and whispered, "Thanks." To get a smile out of Marilyn, he called her "Chubby" or "Fatso" with a pinch on the fanny.

When Marilyn got flustered, she ran off the set to throw up. This meant more delays until she changed her clothes and had her hair and makeup redone. Gable recognized the signs and took her away from the others. "Just take it easy, honey."

"I have problems, you know," she trembled. "I'm so sorry."

"You don't have to apologize to me."

"I could never have gotten through this without you. It's true. Even on the days I was late, the only reason I came at all was to work with you."

"An honor, honey," he said with a grin and a hug. "You know, I've seen some of the rushes and we make a good team. I'd like to make another film with you after I finish *Diamondhead*. How about it?"

"Deal!" she exclaimed. "You won't forget?"

"Honey, I'm the kinda guy who keeps his promises."

Huston said, "Gable looked after Monroe, and Monroe looked after Clift." She remarked that Monty was in worse shape than she was. He was popping pills and drinking grape juice laced with vodka on the set every day. Marilyn nursed his wounds after grueling scenes and she tried to help him with his lines when they worked together. "Monty's like a brother," she said. "I feel very protective when he's around."

Clift usually stayed by himself at night. The few times he went out for dinner, Marilyn was with him. They were two lost children, searching for inner peace and a degree of sanity. Marilyn knew he was gay, or possibly bisexual, but she found Clift to be a very attractive, sensitive and charming man. Elizabeth Taylor fell in love with Monty and was very close to him. How close, Marilyn didn't know. Jealous of Taylor's power and popularity, Marilyn tried to seduce Monty, who had no reaction whatsoever. She described him as "oblivious." But there was no animosity and he was a frequent visitor at her Sutton Place apartment. Marilyn's dilemma was how Elizabeth had managed to share a room with him on location for *Raintree County* only a few years before.

Perhaps Monty was in love with "Bessie," his nickname for Taylor, and perhaps they had their private moments, but MGM knew all about the goings-on. They risked a possible scandal to keep Clift from going over the edge, and Taylor was one person who had a calming influence over him. No one would have believed it, anyway, since Mike Todd's "diamond and emerald" pursuit of Elizabeth made newspaper headlines daily.

Marilyn had a brief affair with Taylor's first husband, Nicky Hilton, but this was no great feat. He was known for his sexual prowess and womanizing.

On October 18, the cast and crew of *The Misfits* left Nevada for Los Angeles where the final close-up shots would be done in the air-conditioned studios at Paramount. Miller wanted more revisions, but Gable said, "I'm finished and no one can do anything to change my mind!" He agreed to one brief scene with Marilyn on November 4 but before saying good-bye, Gable said, "I now have two things to be proud of in my career: *Gone with the Wind* and this."

Marilyn returned to 444 East 57th Street with Arthur, who packed his bags and moved out. He said nothing to her and took nothing that reminded him of their marriage.

On November 17 Marilyn heard the news that Clark Gable was dead. "I loved him," she sobbed to a reporter on the telephone. "He wanted to do another movie with me."

Kay Gable didn't think that was true. In an interview days after her husband's death she said, "It wasn't the physical exertion of *The Misfits* that did it. It was the horrible tension, that eternal waiting, waiting, waiting. He waited for everybody. He'd get so angry waiting that he'd just go ahead and do anything to keep occupied. That's why he did those dangerous stunts."

The press embellished whatever Gable's widow said. It did not take much imagination to blame his death on Marilyn's tardiness and absence during *The Misfits*. The newspapers were brimming over with Clark's patience, kindness and self-control, which eventually erupted in the heart and took his life.

It was the talk of Hollywood because there were witnesses who spoke candidly about Marilyn's lack of consideration.

Marilyn denied the terrible accusations, but was not mentally equipped to deal with them. Bob Slatzer explained to her that Gable began having chest pains after changing a tire on his tractor. "Instead of calling an ambulance, he waited until the following morning. He had no business trying to lift that tractor."

"But you read what Kay said about me."

"Not about you, personally," Slatzer emphasized.

"Who else?" she cried, "Why didn't he say something about my being late? I'd have done anything for him. All he had to do was ask me to be on time. That's all. But he always said, 'That's all right, honey'—like he understood."

Marilyn stayed in bed for weeks, crying and repeating over and over, "I killed him. I did it." The guilt mounted until there was nothing else to do but end the mental anguish. Lena Pepitone found Marilyn about to jump out of the bedroom window and pulled her back. It was mid-December and the city sparkled with Christmas lights and jingle bells. "What have I got to live for?" Marilyn wept.

Pepitone calmed her down and suggested she call Joe DiMaggio. After their phone conversation, Marilyn acted as if she had been reborn.

Kay Gable invited Marilyn to the christening of her son John Clark in March of 1961. The widow apologized for any misunderstanding and said, "Clark never said an unkind word about you."

If there were any doubts that Marilyn was innocent of contributing to Gable's death, they were erased that day she held his son in her arms with glowing pride and deepest affection.

Critics had mixed feelings about *The Misfits*. The *New York Herald-Tribune* said Arthur Miller could not have written it without Marilyn Monroe. The *New York Daily News* thought

Gable and Monroe were at their very best. *Life* magazine said, "Marilyn plays a role into which are written bits and pieces reminiscent of her own life."

Bosley Crowther wrote in the *New York Times*, "There is this to be said for the people that Clark Gable, Marilyn Monroe, *et al* play in John Huston's new film. . . . They are amusing people to be with, for a little while, anyhow. But they are shallow and inconsequential, and that is the dang-busted trouble with this film. . . . Miss Monroe is completely blank and unfathomable. . . . Characters and theme do not congeal. Mr. Gable is ironically vital, but the picture just doesn't come off."

17

Potpourri

Marilyn had not given up on Yves Montand. She expected some response from him when her separation and pending divorce from Miller was announced in November. Reporters flocked to Montand's home in Paris. "Marilyn is a lovely girl," Yves said. "I am so sorry she is divorcing her husband, but I am not leaving my wife."

But the rumors about Marilyn divorcing Arthur to marry Montand persisted. Stories circulated that she had met the Italian several times in Los Angeles during *The Misfits*. It is more logical to believe that Marilyn had spoken to him on the phone after the Idlewild fiasco and he began to weaken. It was Simone who called Marilyn to tell her that Yves had changed his mind about coming to New York. Many Monroe biographers think this final and humiliating rejection from Montand, conveyed by his wife, prompted Marilyn to attempt suicide after Gable's death. Without a doubt she would have had a nervous collapse if it hadn't been for Joe DiMaggio, who came to New York for the Christmas holidays. He usually arrived for dinner, spent the night and left early in the morning, using the service entrance coming and going.

Marilyn was happy with Joe, and she hoped that time would reunite them in marriage. He felt the same way, but was realistic enough to know it could never happen. What bothered him most was her career, but not for selfish reasons any more. Joe knew it was slowly killing her, but he could do nothing more than be there when she needed him.

Marilyn leaned on the Strasbergs, too, and stayed at their apartment on Central Park West if she didn't want to be alone. Having lost faith in Paula, Marilyn spent time with Lee Strasberg, to whom she left the bulk of her estate in a new will drawn up in January of 1961. This sudden urge to get her affairs in order was not taken lightly by her few close friends, but she shrugged it off as the thing to do when one gets a divorce.

It was decided by her press agents that Marilyn should fly to Juarez, Mexico, for a divorce on the day of John F. Kennedy's inauguration to avoid publicity. On January 20, she requested a divorce on the grounds of "incompatibility of character," but the newspapers gave Marilyn Monroe's divorce priority over President John F. Kennedy's oath of office.

The last straw in a series of blighted hopes for Marilyn was the disappointment of *The Misfits* that opened in New York on February 2, 1961. If the critics had anything good to say it was out of respect for Clark Gable and the genius of director Huston.

Marilyn was also depressed over the death of Miller's mother, Augusta. "The last time I saw her she begged me not to divorce Arthur. Why couldn't it have been under happier circumstances?"

Unable to sleep, Marilyn began popping more pills than usual and drinking to excess. She told a close friend that she almost jumped from the living room window and then thought better of it "because there was a woman in a brown dress standing near the awning of my building and I knew her. So I came back inside. It was frustrating."

Marilyn had often said her pill overdoses were not deliberate.

Craving some sleep, she forgot how many capsules she had taken and how far apart. But in February of 1961 Marilyn was terrified it might happen again and, if so, Arthur would not be there to save her. She related this fear to her psychiatrist and asked to be admitted to a hospital where she might get some rest without relying on pills and booze. This was a logical request, but Marilyn also told Dr. Kris about her attempts to jump from the thirteenth floor of her apartment building. Without hesitation, Dr. Kris admitted Marilyn to the Payne-Witney Psychiatric Clinic where she was locked in a room on a floor for mentally disturbed patients.

Marilyn's version of what happened differs from that of the nurses and doctors. She said, "I was drugged and tied down to the bed. People came to look at me through the bars. I screamed for them to let me out—that I didn't belong there." She wrote a desperate note to the Strasbergs, begging them to get in touch with Dr. Kris. Marilyn was sure Lee would do something to help her, but he did nothing. After four days she was finally allowed to call DiMaggio in Florida. He got on the next plane to New York and physically took Marilyn out of Payne-Whitney and checked her into Columbia Presbyterian Medical Center. During her three weeks there, she was gradually taken off drugs until she was able to sleep without medication.

Bob Slatzer said there was a conspiracy to keep Marilyn confined to an institution: "Lee Strasberg was calling the shots. He told Dr. Kris what to do. When Marilyn found out, she was afraid Strasberg would have her committed since she had no one else. She never trusted him again, but she never got around to changing her will, either. Aside from small bequests, Marilyn left twenty-five percent to Dr. Kris, a trust for her mother and the rest to Lee Strasberg. As it turned out, Marilyn's estate was in the red when she died."

Slatzer had married and divorced twice. One of his wives was extremely jealous when Marilyn called. "That didn't help my shaky marriage," he said. "Marilyn thought the whole thing was silly and phoned anyway. If I was in New York, she usually wanted to meet me some place and talk, sometimes we'd stroll through Central Park. She often reminisced about our brief marriage and wondered if we should try again, but we'd both been through too much. Above all, we wanted to hold on to our deep-rooted friendship, and marriage has a way of destroying that forever."

It was on the set of *The Misfits* when Marilyn found out there was another woman in Miller's life. She thought he was having an affair, but suspected the wrong girl. Arthur claimed he was not involved with thirty-seven-year-old Ingeborg Morath, an Austrian-born freelance photographer, who had been assigned to take pictures on location of *The Misfits*. Yet the romance resumed when he ran into her on Fifth Avenue in New York. (They were married in February of 1962.) The courtship was reported by the news media, which hinted it was Miller's infidelity that broke up his marriage to Marilyn. However, she was supposedly flying to Los Angeles to be with Yves Montand. Although these rumors persisted, there had to be some truth in what events were to follow.

While Marilyn was being linked to Yves Montand, a revealing and historical article appeared in the *Los Angeles Times* on November 9, 1960. Art Buchwald penned the famous and amusing "Monroe Doctrine," asking whether John Kennedy's first order of business in January, after he was sworn in, would be Marilyn Monroe now that she was divorcing Arthur Miller. Buchwald was one of very few journalists to expose the relationship between the Sex Goddess and the President-elect.

Who floundered most, Monroe or Kennedy, might have been an interesting contest but no one cared at the time. All eyes were on the frail and elegant debutante First Lady, Jacqueline Kennedy. Americans adored the beautiful young couple, living in what she described as "Camelot." How could the President possibly be interested in another woman?

He wasn't. He was interested in many, many women and Monroe was merely one of them.

Kennedy was only one of Marilyn's lovers, too. She needed sex to renew her confidence after being rejected by Montand. Aside from the President, there was Frank Sinatra, who gave her a dog she called Mafia, much to his dismay. And DiMaggio when he was in New York. But not all the men around Marilyn were famous. The housekeeper could not help but hear Marilyn's giggles when she was alone with her good-looking masseur. Then there was an Italian chauffeur that Marilyn requested if she needed a limousine. He came to her apartment on Sutton Place when she stayed home, too.

Henry Rosenfeld, a wealthy New York dress manufacturer, had known Marilyn since she was a starlet. Theirs was an intimate relationship, but she also trusted Henry and confided in him over the years. He helped Marilyn financially when she was setting up her own production company. She referred to Rosenfeld as her financial advisor, but it was so typical of Marilyn not to take his or anyone else's advice. He proposed marriage, but she wasn't in love with Henry.

Jack Cole, who had choreographed Marilyn's dance routines in *Gentlemen Prefer Blondes* and *Let's Make Love*, was popular with Hollywood actresses, with whom he had many affairs. Cole told author John Kobal (*People Will Talk*), "Monroe was screamingly beautiful. She looked like the kind of person who would say, 'Can I use your pool to take a sunning?' and then get your pants off in about six minutes." Cole apparently did not always coddle Marilyn who, he said, complained during a scene in *Let's Make Love* that she had nothing to do. "Then stick your finger up your ass," he said. "I think that's quite within the realm of your technical facilities." Later Cole apologized and when the film was finished, Marilyn gave him a check for $2,000 and reminded him that they had a date in New York.

*

Marilyn was involved with Yul Brynner, whose son Rock said he woke up one morning and found her clothes strewn around the house. Rock met the naked Marilyn in his father's bedroom, where she had spent the night. Brynner was known for his sexual prowess with many, many women, including Judy Garland, Ingrid Bergman, Joan Crawford and Marlene Dietrich.

Marilyn's steamy reputation had her in bed with columnist Walter Winchell and gangster Bugsy Siegel. But the most persistent gossip was about her supposed lesbianism that, rumor had it, began with the very close relationship with Natasha Lytess, as well as an alleged affair with a well-known actress at the Studio Club in Hollywood. Twentieth Century-Fox paid off a woman who threatened to expose her affair with Marilyn. Whether the studio was trying to avoid a nuisance lawsuit or had proof that the lesbian was telling the truth, isn't known.

More than one of Marilyn's close associates think she was intimate with her psychiatrist, Dr. Greenson. No one wished to be quoted because their assumptions were drawn only from what Marilyn said in passing. A psychiatrist who has an affair with his patient, usually a result of an attraction caused by "transference," is highly unethical even if both are consenting. It is frowned upon even in the loosest society because the mind is more fragile than the body and the results more debilitating. We'll never know if there was anything between Marilyn and Greenson. Tapes of his sessions with her still existed when he died in 1978.

Greenson was criticized by his peers, anyway, for inviting Marilyn into his home and welcoming her as a close friend of the family. Their sessions were usually late in the day at his house, and she often stayed for cocktails and dinner. Greenson said Marilyn needed family surroundings and she enjoyed the company of his wife and children.

When she wasn't in Los Angeles, Marilyn called Greenson

every day, sometimes several times a day. "We're always in touch," she said. "I can't live without him." Her deep feelings could have been misinterpreted by those friends who knew only too well that Marilyn had to go all the way with any man she adored as much as Dr. Greenson. And she enjoyed giving the impression that it was true.

Marilyn's dress designer Billy Travilla was her dear friend and occasional lover. David Conover, who discovered and photographed Marilyn on the assembly line at the war factory in 1944, stayed in touch with her over the years and claims they had an affair. Her distinguished agent Charlie Feldman and director Nicholas Ray were her lovers for a brief time, also.

Marilyn's habit of not wearing any clothes at home or in her dressing room explains many of her dalliances. Natasha Lytess said, "Being naked seemed to soothe her." Marilyn told Bob Slatzer about a recurring dream: "I'm in church, listening to a sermon, and all of a sudden I stand up and I'm perfectly nude. I wanted desperately to appear naked for God."

Slatzer said, "That's pure narcissism."

"What's that?"

"It means self-love. That's why you spend so much time standing in front of those full-length mirrors."

"Is that bad?" she asked.

"Not as far as I'm concerned. Most people do the same thing, but won't admit it."

"I don't know about everybody," she giggled, "but my body is my 'magic friend.'"

Slatzer had seen Marilyn parade nude at private parties, knowing she was not trying to seduce anyone. It was attention and adoration she wanted.

But how many men, who saw her every day when she was working on a film, could be objective? As a tribute to herself, she gave them the pleasure of going all the way. It was a perfectly natural gesture on Marilyn's part and accepted as such by the men on her staff.

With the exception of Yves Montand, she was not romantically involved with her leading men. This is extraordinary, considering the sexual magnetism of Robert Mitchum, who might have responded if Joe DiMaggio hadn't been around. Rory Calhoun was irresistible to women, but he was not one of Marilyn's men.

In 1961, Bob Slatzer decided to write Marilyn's biography. They had discussed his doing it and she was agreeable. He specifically wanted to gather her observations about the men in her life.

"Who was the most fascinating man you ever met?" he asked.

"Nikita Khrushchev is one," she replied, "but I think Carl Sandburg is even more interesting."

"What about the men you dated, excluding spouses."

"If it matters, Jim Dougherty was my favorite husband."

Slatzer thought that was interesting, but wondered if it was the champagne talking. They were in the famed Cinegrill at the Hollywood Roosevelt Hotel, sitting in a dark corner booth, making it difficult for him to study her mood.

Without pondering Marilyn said, "The most fascinating man I ever dated was Frank Sinatra."

"Why didn't you ever mention him?"

"You asked me, and I'm telling you, so just take notes," she said bluntly. "Frank has always been kind and understanding. When I'm with him, I feel like I don't have to take pills. He makes me feel secure and happy. He makes me laugh. He's the only man who's taught me how to love life. He's really a gentleman."

"Did you think he was a gentleman the night he broke down that door with Joe?"

"I think Frankie was mad because I wouldn't do *Pink Tights*. He was getting more money, but the real reason was Joe. He didn't want me to work with Frankie."

"Do you want to discuss Yves Montand?" Bob asked.

"Oh, that was a great romance," she replied. "He [Yves] was like Frank Sinatra—a very sensitive, nice person and very sexy."

"Who else?"

"I had a special fondness for Billie Daniels. He coached me to sing 'That Old Black Magic' in *Bus Stop*. I used to call him in the middle of the night and he invited me over. So I'd go to Billie's place and stay until daylight."

Marilyn talked about the men who helped her get started in films, but found it difficult to discuss Johnny Hyde for any length of time. "We'll continue on another day," she said.

Slatzer never finished her biography because she died eight months later. Instead he wrote *The Life and Curious Death of Marilyn Monroe* in 1974. This book led to further investigation into Marilyn's "suicide" that continues to this day.

Marilyn hoped to marry Frank Sinatra. Though she rented a house in Beverly Hills "to give Liz Taylor a run for her money," and get back into the mainstream of the Hollywood rat race, one very good reason for wanting to be there was Sinatra, who preferred Los Angeles. Marilyn was willing to live there if they got married, but once again she was dreaming about the impossible, building up the romance and translating Frank's endearing words into what she wanted to believe. He had, for some time, preferred not being seen with Marilyn in public other than her attending his shows in Las Vegas and Reno. But she was seated with his other friends at a ringside table and the press did not take much notice. It's unlikely Sinatra was concerned about DiMaggio's feelings, but he was eager to impress Jack Kennedy, whose trysts with Marilyn were beginning to be well known in Hollywood and Washington.

In September of 1961, Frank invited her to a formal benefit. Marilyn was thrilled to be seen with him in public and she surmised this was the buildup to his proposing marriage. Marilyn was sure of it when he gave her a pair of emerald earrings.

"Oh, they're beautiful!" she gasped.

"They should be," he said. "They cost me thirty-five thousand dollars."

They were a steady couple for a while, but Frank preferred staying out of the limelight. Though Marilyn claimed she didn't need pills during this romantic interlude, she was in a constant daze that was apparent to everyone who socialized with them.

Marilyn returned to New York, hoping Frank would miss her enough to propose marriage. He called her faithfully and she played his records night and day. Then word got around that Frank was dating twenty-four-year-old Juliet Prowse, a beautiful dancer from South Africa.

Marilyn fell into another state of depression. She was feeling "very old" because Sinatra had chosen to be with a younger woman. But she said nothing to him on the phone, and they dated when she returned to Los Angeles. Her feelings for Frank hadn't changed, because she realized he did not want to be tied down or get married again.

Yet Sinatra became engaged to Juliet Prowse in January of 1962. She refused to give up her career and he broke off their engagement a month later. Dorothy Kilgallen wrote in her column that the whole thing was a publicity stunt: "Miss Prowse was making $500 a week in Las Vegas before she met Frank Sinatra. Now she's getting $17,500!"

By the end of 1961, even though Dr. Greenson was optimistic, Marilyn was severely on the decline. The information that he later divulged deals primarily with her sexual hang-ups, loneliness and dependency on drugs. He said that Marilyn was unable to have orgasms with one man for any length of time. This is interesting because Marilyn, by her own admission, had never achieved an orgasm. She told Bob Slatzer it was fun telling fibs to her psychiatrists and that she never told them everything.

Obviously, Marilyn wanted Greenson to believe she was able to reach a climax if for no other reason than to prove to him she was a "complete woman."

Author Anthony Summers obtained correspondence from Greenson to a colleague about Marilyn, indicating it was almost impossible to separate their personal friendship from their professional relationship. Greenson complained that she cancelled several appointments with him to be with Sinatra in Palm Springs. "She is unfaithful to me as one is to a parent. . . . "

Greenson also concluded that Marilyn had a dreaded fear of anything lesbian, but was drawn into situations of "homosexual coloring." She hired and then fired a housekeeper who resembled Natasha Lytess, and became suspicious of attentive women.

Marilyn began to thrive on one-night stands with men she had never met before and would never see again. They were usually well-built jocks who never dreamed they would ever meet Marilyn Monroe, much less go to bed with her. If she was truthful about having these flings, there was surely a pattern that dated back to when Jim Dougherty was overseas and she picked up men in bars.

"I was happy because I made them happy," Marilyn said.

18

Jack

Marilyn had met Senator John F. Kennedy in 1954 at a party given by agent (and former lover) Charles Feldman at his home in Beverly Hills. Kennedy wanted to meet her and asked his brother-in-law actor Peter Lawford to arrange it. Nothing happened between them that evening because Jackie Kennedy was furious when she caught her husband staring at Marilyn, and Joe DiMaggio was alerted, too. He disliked "Jack" Kennedy right away and wanted to leave the party. Joe and Marilyn argued until he literally "dragged" her out of Feldman's house.

The thirty-seven-year-old senator from Massachusetts had quite a reputation with women even after his 1953 marriage to debutante Jacqueline Lee Bouvier. In social and political circles, this union was accepted as an arrangement more than a love match. The Kennedys had wealth, but could not enter the Social Register because Irish Catholics were not considered eligible. Having a Bouvier in the family gave them the stature that money could not provide.

Jack's father, Joe Kennedy, made his money in banking, the motion picture industry and real estate. A man of great vigor and drive, he settled in Boston, married the mayor's daughter, and was appointed U.S. ambassador to Great Britain. Joe had a delicious wit and was an outrageous flirt. When he offered to help couturier Oleg Cassini, whose courtship of Grace Kelly was wobbly after her parents rejected him, Joe referred to Oleg as a "donkey" and tried to make a date with Grace! "We Irish have to stick together." He winked.

Later, Jack liked to embarrass Cassini at informal White House gatherings by asking him to tell the story "about how Dad screwed you up with Grace Kelly."

In the late twenties Joe spent a good deal of his time in Hollywood, where he met and fell in love with actress Gloria Swanson. Since divorce was impossible, he wanted the spunky Gloria to be his mistress, and boldly took her on an ocean voyage to Europe aboard the same ship as his wife and sister "because you'll have to meet them sometime."

It wasn't only romance and moonlight for Joe and Gloria. He set up an independent production company with the intention of financing her films, but he walked out on a flop and left Gloria with all the unpaid bills. Almost as sad, she lost her titled husband, the Marquis de la Falaise, for the love of Joseph Kennedy.

Jack was a chip off the old block when it came to women. He wasn't sure what he wanted to be when he grew up, but fate stepped in when his eldest brother, Joe Jr., was killed in World War II. The elder Kennedy's dream was seeing one of his three sons in the White House. Since Jack was next in line, he was groomed for politics. He graduated from Harvard in 1940, joined the Navy and took part in operations against the Japanese in the southwest Pacific. After his PT boat was rammed by an enemy destroyer, he was invalided home and discharged in 1945.

When Jack was twenty-nine, he ran for Congress on the Democratic ticket and entered the House of Representatives in January of 1947. Five years later he defeated Republican incumbent Henry Cabot Lodge to graduate to the Senate.

Jack's brother Robert, eight years younger, also graduated

from Harvard and then the University of Virginia law school in 1951. He entered public service as an attorney for the criminal division of the US Department of Justice, resigning to manage Jack's campaign for the Senate.

There were five Kennedy sisters. Kathleen was killed in a plane crash in 1948; Rosemary suffered from mental retardation; Eunice married R. Sargent Shriver, Jr., the first director of the Peace Corps; Jean married Stephen E. Smith; and Patricia married actor Peter Lawford in 1954.

The Kennedy clan believed in the notion "all for one and one for all." They supported each other at election time, dinnertime and playtime. While they romped at touch fooball, Jackie Bouvier Kennedy read a book. While they ate hot dogs, she nibbled on cucumber sandwiches. It was difficult getting her on the campaign trail, but when she did, Jack walked in her shadow and enjoyed every minute of it.

Joe Kennedy was outraged when his daughter Pat married actor Peter Lawford, who was never completely welcomed into the Kennedy clan. But Pat's money made it possible for them to purchase an elaborate Santa Monica beach house owned by his former MGM boss, Louis B. Mayer.

Jack liked to watch the pretty bikini-clad girls walking on the beach. Peter made sure that his brother-in-law had the pick of the litter at house parties, and was known around Hollywood as "Kennedy's pimp."

Jack will not go down in history as a great lover, preferring quantity to quality. One of his chauffeurs said, "Kennedy was like the rooster in a hen house. Bam, bam, bam. At a party, Jack took a girl in the library, sat her on a desk, pulled up her dress and it was over. She didn't know they started! He came out and looked around the room for another girl. I was constantly reminding him to 'zip up.' "

Senator George Smathers said, "No one was off limits to Jack—not your wife, your mother or your sister. Having two girls at once was one of his favorite pastimes."

"If I go too long without sex," Kennedy told British Prime Minister Harold Macmillan, "I get headaches. Dad wanted all his boys to get laid as often as possible, but I'm never through with a girl until I've had her three ways."

Jack told Clare Boothe Luce, "I'm not the tragic lover type."

It would be too time consuming to mention the many women in Kennedy's life, and it's doubtful anyone knows or kept count. His political career was almost ruined before it began when Jack had an affair with Danish journalist Inge Arvad, a suspected Nazi spy. The elder Kennedy used his influence in Washington, and this explosive episode was hushed up.

Whether Jack was just happy-go-lucky or knew his family had the power and money to get him out of trouble, he went on his merry way with little, if any, discretion. When pictures were taken of him leaving the Georgetown apartment of his secretary, Pam Turnure, with whom he was having an affair, the young senator laughed it off. The newspapers would not use them and Joe Kennedy refused to "pay off." Amazingly, Kennedy got Pam a job as Jackie's press secretary at the White House!

Jack had flings with stripper Blaze Starr, painter Mary Pinchot Meyer, and actresses Jayne Mansfield, Gene Tierney, Lee Remick and Angie Dickinson. One of Jack's favorites was lovely Judith Campbell (née Exner), whose Mafia connections caused a good deal of publicity following Kennedy's death.

Judith complained that one night when Jack invited her to his suite at the Beverly Hilton Hotel, she found him in bed with a pretty black girl. Jack invited her to "hop in" and join them, but Judith stormed out of the room.

While Kennedy was recuperating from back surgery after Feldman's party, a poster of Marilyn was taped to a wall where he could admire it. His affair with her began early in 1955 after Marilyn's divorce from DiMaggio and continued throughout her marriage to Arthur Miller. She and Jack arranged to meet at Lawford's house or out-of-the-way Malibu motels. In New York, it was the Carlyle Hotel. Marilyn said, in jest, that she frequently made love to Jack for therapeutic reasons. "He has a bad back." She giggled. "I made him feel better."

Many women said Kennedy's lying on his back made them feel as if they were there to "service" him. He made no promises nor did he buy expensive gifts for women with the exception of Judith Campbell, who wrote in her memoirs that Jack wanted to buy her a fur coat. The twenty-six-year-old brunette "starlet" refused the mink, but accepted a diamond and ruby brooch.

Frank Sinatra introduced Jack to the beautiful Judith in February 1960 at the Sands Hotel in Las Vegas. Frank also introduced her to underworld figure Sam Giancana, and she had simultaneous affairs with two of the most powerful men in the world.

Kennedy was obviously captivated by Judith because he sent roses and called her every day before the affair began at the Plaza Hotel in New York. When he was elected President, she often met him at the White House.

There are two schools of thought as to why Kennedy showed more interest in Miss Campbell than he did in other women, including Marilyn Monroe. Either Jack was stuck on Judith or he was using her as a conduit to CIA-Mafia plotter Sam Giancano, attempting to arrange the assassination of Fidel Castro. Jack stopped seeing Judith when FBI chief J. Edgar Hoover told Kennedy that he knew about the Campbell affair and her link to the underworld. Knowing Hoover was prepared to destroy him, Kennedy broke away from Judith, who resented being dumped and then hounded by the FBI as soon as Jack was out of danger.

The Judith Campbell affair is particularly significant because John Kennedy walked away unscathed from this politically damaging situation into another with Marilyn. Her relationship with Jack was sporadic in the fifties, but became intense on her part when he became a candidate for president in 1959. She campaigned for him and was seen at a Los Angeles political rally with another supporter, Sammy Davis, Jr. By now, her romance with Kennedy was taken for granted by insiders, but as one of his colleagues said, "Marilyn Monroe is just another cup of coffee to Jack." Yet she was one of the few women whose affair with him lasted as long as it did.

Judith Campbell said in an interview for *People* magazine (1988) that Kennedy told her in 1960, "If I don't win the Democratic nomination for president, Jackie and I are getting a divorce." A rumor persists to this day that Joseph Kennedy gave Jackie one million dollars to stay with Jack. Surprisingly, she was in love with him despite her playing third fiddle to politics and other women. They eventually shared an understanding—a blending of friendship, love for their children and pride in each other's public image on the political front. It wasn't Camelot, but they had their moments.

The women who thought Kennedy might marry them, including Marilyn, were living in a dream world. The beautiful actress Gene Tierney dated Jack in 1946 when he was a bachelor and she was separated from couturier Oleg Cassini. Miss Tierney fell in love with Mr. Kennedy and they had a lovely romance that lasted about a year. It was at lunch one day that he looked at her and said, out of the blue, "You know, Gene, I can never marry you." Stunned more by his timing than his announcement, Gene did not respond. But when lunch was over she said, "Bye, bye, Jack!" His attempts to see Gene again failed.

Miss Tierney verified that Jack was not one to send flowers or buy expensive gifts. What Kennedy gave was his charm and wit, and he had an abundance of both. Peter Lawford said, "Of all Jack's women, I think Marilyn complemented him most. They both had a sense of humor that clicked." Also, Marilyn was a woman who did not seek or expect sexual gratification. She was a playful bed partner for Jack who enjoyed prolonging the fun if, that is, he had the time. At Lawford's Santa Monica house Kennedy was at his leisure even when he became President. It seemed perfectly logical that Jack would prefer relaxing at his sister's well-guarded beach mansion rather than a hotel.

Bob Slatzer recalls Marilyn's comparing the brothers Kennedy: "Jack always carried a stack of books with him when he left the White House. He was an ardent reader and liked to discuss art, Greek tragedies, drama and even Hollywood gossip. All Bobby ever talked about was his work. It was hard for him to relax."

Since Jackie Kennedy's territory was the East Coast and she very rarely accompanied her husband to California, Marilyn decided to make her home base in Los Angeles.

19

The Prez

Dr. Greenson urged Marilyn to buy a house in Hollywood because she needed the security of her own home, and a housekeeper-companion, as well. Mrs. Eunice Murray* said, "Dr. Greenson was a friend of mine and he asked me to visit Marilyn and get acquainted. My first assignment was to go house-hunting with her. She wanted a 'Mexican' style place like Dr. Greenson's. We found an unpretentious one on Fifth Helena Drive in Brentwood for less than ninety thousand dollars. I think she put one half down and took out a mortgage for the rest."

The single-story, white stucco house, built in 1928, was surrounded by multicolored flowers, vines and thick green foliage. A small guest house and garage, jutting out into an "L", were under the same red-tile roof as the main house. There was a spacious living room decorated all in white, with natural hewn beams, a fireplace, three bedrooms and a sun room that led to the garden and an oval swimming pool.

An old inscription on the stone wall near the front door read, CURSUM PERFICIO: "I'm completing my journey . . . "

---

* Mrs. Murray denied at the time that she was anything more than a seamstress-housekeeper. Actually, she was a psychiatric nurse cognizant of patients with psychological problems, and had previously worked for Dr. Greenson before, "disguising" herself as a housekeeper.

Of course, the place was ideally located. In a matter of minutes Marilyn could drive to Dr. Greenson's home or Peter Lawford's beach house.

What did Patricia Kennedy Lawford think about her brother's meetings with the Sex Goddess? She was used to his womanizing and thought nothing of it. There was no love lost between the Kennedy girls and Jackie, anyway.

Peter liked Marilyn, but was turned off on their first date in the early fifties. When he picked her up, he was disgusted by the dog waste in her living room. While Peter waited for Marilyn, he tried to clean up the smelly mess and was so sick to his stomach during dinner, he asked someone else to take Marilyn home. Peter remarked to a friend that he could never go to bed with a woman who lived in such filth.

Marilyn's housekeepers were also appalled by her lack of personal hygiene. She would sometimes go for a week or more without taking a shower or combing her hair, and wore the same old white terry cloth robe if she put on anything at all. In direct contrast, Marilyn might take two baths if she had a date and redo her makeup four or five times before showing up a few hours late. When she wasn't working, Marilyn couldn't be bothered with makeup or having her hair bleached, allowing the dark roots to be exposed. What she did in the privacy of her own home is relatively unimportant, but Marilyn often gave interviews in this unkempt state. Jack Cole said she occasionally came to rehearsals looking disheveled and wearing a skimpy outfit that left nothing to the imagination. Cole said, "Damn it, Marilyn, haven't you got any pride! Do something with yourself." But she was oblivious. It was a touchy subject, and few people had the nerve to say anything.

Former lover James Bacon was doing a story on Marilyn and went to her dressing room during rehearsals for *River of No Return*. "She looked like Dracula's daughter," he remarked. "I was in a state of shock." Bacon said he often had to wait hours while she transformed herself from Norma Jeane into Marilyn.

This was a ritual when she was virtually unknown and when she was a star. "It's pathetic, in retrospect," Bacon said.

But it was always and none other than Marilyn Monroe in the company of John F. Kennedy, whom she called "The Prez." He never went to her new Brentwood house for both reasons of propriety and security. Jack frequently met Marilyn at Bing Crosby's place in Palm Springs. Wearing a brown wig and glasses, she was flown in a private plane or Air Force One, depending on the destination. Lawford passed off Marilyn as his secretary. "You have to take notes," he said. She was annoyed if Peter gave dictation at length, calling him foul names under her breath. Regardless, the intrigue added a good deal of excitement to what she considered a top-rate and romantic affair with the President of the United States.

It's never been suggested that Marilyn met Jack at the White House, but Mickey Rooney mentioned in his 1991 memoirs that he was listening to Kennedy make a speech in the Rose Garden when he spotted Marilyn. "Jeez!" Rooney wrote. "Does he do it with Marilyn in the White House?"

Rooney said it was no secret about the affair, but he was rather surprised to see her at a White House function.

Marilyn had Jack's private phone number and called him at will. Occasionally, Jackie answered and handed the receiver to her husband, who wasn't the least bit concerned until Marilyn called Jackie personally and confronted the First Lady about giving her husband a divorce. Jacqueline Kennedy was livid, but it was beneath her to show her true feelings. She said Jack could have his freedom, but reminded Marilyn that she would have to live in the White House, often referred to as "The Glass House" by Jackie who understood the strain of it all too well. She knew Marilyn would not be able to deal with this emotionally.

In her attempt to force Jack into making a choice, Marilyn gave him another good reason to break off the relationship.

There is no doubt that Peter Lawford knew more about this

notorious and never-to-be-forgotten affair than most. But he was drinking heavily and into dope and pills, making for an unreliable source. He told many conflicting stories and many different versions of these stories. Lawford was a weak fellow at his best. He often found himself in the middle of difficult situations such as making arrangements for Jack Kennedy to stay at Frank Sinatra's estate in Palm Springs only to find out the President changed his mind because Frank had Mafia connections—Sam Giancana, in particular. When Ol' Blue Eyes found out Jack was staying at Bing Crosby's place instead, he blamed Lawford, who, until then was a privileged member of Sinatra's "Rat Pack." Frank never spoke to Peter again. Kennedy could have explained the situation to his pal Sinatra who had been a faithful campaigner and supporter. Peter took the rap instead, and continued to allow the Kennedys to use him. One of his duties was driving Marilyn to Crosby's place in Palm Springs. Jack was not above inviting carefully selected friends for cocktails and greeting them with a tipsy Marilyn at his side. She was never all together on these occasions. One has to wonder why Kennedy would expose her so blatantly unless he wanted to prove they were sharing the same bed in Crosby's desert retreat.

Philip Watson, who was running for Los Angeles County Assessor on the Democratic ticket, told author Anthony Summers that he had attended a party at the Beverly Hilton Hotel* several months earlier and saw the President with Marilyn. Watson wasn't surprised to see them together again, but he was somewhat embarrassed that Jack chose to entertain guests in the cottage he was sharing with Marilyn. Watson said, "She was wearing only a robe and it was obvious she'd had too much to drink."

In the early months of 1962, Marilyn believed she would be

---

* Jack maintained the Presidential Suite at the Beverly Hilton Hotel.

Jack's wife after his first term in office. She confided this to a few friends, including Lawford, who knew it would never happen. He understood his brother-in-law only too well, but he listened to Marilyn's fantasy and said nothing. Peter had not been concerned about her well-being because she'd been around and knew the consequences of having affairs with married men. Actually, Lawford did not fully comprehend the seriousness of Marilyn's instability. So many in his crowd drank too much, smoked marijuana, tried LSD, took a variety of pills and bed-hopped.

Lawford had been in Hollywood for twenty years. Abused by his nanny when he was ten, Peter was plagued by sexual hang-ups that blossomed during his marriage to Patricia Kennedy. In his heyday as one of MGM's most popular leading men, during World War II, he almost married Lana Turner, dated Ava Gardner and Rita Hayworth, and was involved with Judy Garland, who relied on stimulants and sedatives for survival.

Peter supplied Marilyn with an assortment of prescription drugs and they sometimes injected themselves for a speedier effect. It was suspected that Marilyn was on hard drugs when a syringe and needle were found in her bathroom, but there has never been evidence that she went any further than trying something for the sheer fun of it. During the last six months of her life, Marilyn was taking hormone shots to slow down the aging process, a common practice in Hollywood.

Subconsciously, Marilyn, the woman, knew that John Kennedy was only interested in Marilyn, the movie goddess. For fear of losing him, she could not allow Norma Jeane to surface. Her relationship with the President was a worse strain on her than facing the camera. Dr. Greenson remarked, "The main mechanism she used to bring some feeling of stability and significance to her life was the attractiveness of her body."

If Jack stayed at the beach house for any length of time, Marilyn moved in, also. She envied Pat's life with Peter, not knowing the marriage was essentially over and that he was seeing other women. Jack enjoyed comparing notes with his brother-in-law about their intimate affairs, each trying to outdo the other.

At Kennedy's request, Peter took pictures of him making love to Marilyn in the Lawfords' marble-and-onyx bathtub. Jack's "turn-on" was a snapshot of her performing fellatio on him.

But Lawford wasn't the only one recording these private interludes. His house and telephone had been bugged in 1961 by Jimmy Hoffa's master eavesdropper Bernard Spindel to tape conversations of the Kennedy brothers. The voice, sighs and giggles of Marilyn Monroe were a bonus. As a result, her cozy hacienda was wired, too.

Joe DiMaggio was also keeping tabs on Marilyn. Reliable sources claim he knew of her activities and her whereabouts.

But DiMaggio's "concern" was harmless compared to Jimmy Hoffa's hatred for Attorney General Robert Kennedy, who was determined to put the Teamster boss behind bars.

Jack, who had turned on Sam Giancana and the Mafia, was in worse danger. FBI Chief J. Edgar Hoover warned Kennedy about Judith Campbell and she was promptly dumped. But within weeks Jack was seeing Marilyn. Did he really think the big boys would let bygones be bygones? Could he have been so innocent as to believe that if he was no longer intimate with Giancana's girlfriend, he was safe in bed with Marilyn Monroe?

It was Hoover's pleasure to inform the Kennedy brothers of impending scandals because, indirectly, it was a warning to them that he knew more than he was telling. If they still had any thoughts of replacing him, Hoover wanted them to know he had the upper hand.

Jack continued his sexual antics, but brother Bobby was very concerned over information passed on to him by Justice Department officials and the FBI. Before the President got himself into more trouble, Bobby intervened.

20

Bobby

Bobby Kennedy was a year older than Marilyn. He had been married to Ethel Skakel Kennedy for more than a decade and had seven children. Bobby was described by John Davis, author of *The Kennedys*, as "a classic puritan, moralistic and wholly committed to the work effort." He believed in getting up early in the morning, then working uninterrupted until he virtually dropped from exhaustion at the end of the day.

Bobby was a more dedicated politician than John and Edward Kennedy, but he *was* his father's son. Rather than affairs, he had brief flings with young girls including Jayne Mansfield, a hand-me-down of Jack's. The Kennedy boys were known for sharing or giving their girlfriends to each other. There were few rumors about Bobby's romances, however.

How and when he met Marilyn cannot be verified. Wilbur Clark, manager of the Desert Inn Casino and Hotel in Las Vegas, said Bobby got her there every few weeks as far back as 1957. Jimmy Hoffa's foster son, Chuck O'Brien, claims that Marilyn was involved with Bobby in the late fifties. When asked how he got this information, O'Brien said it was Hoffa's business to know everything about Robert Kennedy. Wilbur Clark was quoted as saying, "He's been screwing around with her for a long time." Though these testimonies seem farfetched, they are worth mentioning because Marilyn and Bobby were intimate while she was still seeing Jack. She said the first time Bobby made love to her was in a car outside Lawford's beach house. Regardless of the time element, "The Prez" was sharing her with his brother.

Jack was more interested in another woman, anyway. She was the very beautiful blonde socialite Mary Pinchot Meyer, ex-wife of high-ranking CIA official Cord Meyer. She was forty-two, came from a wealthy family, graduated from Vassar, and was a friend of Jackie's. Mary was adventurous, witty, worldly and bright. Jack's affair with her began in January of 1962 and lasted until his death.

While Marilyn was popping pills and drinking champagne to forget Jack, he was smoking marijuana and trying LSD in the White House bedroom with Mary. If Jackie was in town, the lovers met at Mary's place in nearby Georgetown.

Soon after Kennedy's assassination, Mary was shot in the head while she was jogging on the towpath along the Potomac River. The killer has never been found. Mary's diary, containing details of her affair with the president, was destroyed by the CIA.

Bobby objected to his brother's nude swimming parties at the White House and was appalled to hear about naked women running around, but he never criticized Jack or tried to discourage him from having fun. Instead Bobby fiercely defended his brother. A Kennedy aide said, "Bobby was a real square. He objected to vulgarity and improper conduct in the family. Such a prude! At a White House party, he stormed on the dance floor because he thought writer Gore Vidal was holding Jackie too close and broke it up. He finally told Vidal off. Jackie thought the whole thing was silly, but thanked Bobby for his gallantry."

It was with the same gallantry, apparently, that Bobby got caught up in a web with Marilyn. Going to bed with him at the outset was her way of ingratiating herself into the Kennedy family for the love of Jack.

Peter Lawford, who hoped to get a rise out of Bobby, seated him between Marilyn and Kim Novak at a dinner party in April of 1961. Later that evening, Bobby and Marilyn went off in a corner by themselves and were deep in conversation. Knowing he was the intellectual type, she boned up on social issues that interested him. These notes might have been the first in a so-called diary that was meant to help her remember their political discussions " … so he won't think I'm stupid," she told Bob Slatzer.

Though Bobby was obviously attracted to Marilyn, Peter could not possibly have expected anything compared to a similar dinner when Jack put his hand under the table to feel Marilyn's thigh and went up too far. When he discovered she was wearing nothing underneath her dress, Jack actually blushed.

Though Bobby took life very seriously and had little time for silly escapades, Marilyn's good friend Jeanne Carmen remembers answering the door in the late summer of 1961 and seeing none other than the Attorney General of the United States standing there looking a bit shy. Marilyn ran into his arms and kissed him on the lips.

"We dared Bobby to go with us to a nude beach," Carmen said. "He took the dare and we fixed him up with a false beard, baseball cap and sunglasses. We walked along the beach and sat on a blanket for a while. Here were two famous people that nobody recognized. We laughed about it all the way home."

In December of that year, the elder Kennedy suffered a stroke and Marilyn apparently sent a "Get Well" note to Joe, whom she'd met when Jack was campaigning in Los Angeles. Supposedly Jean Kennedy Smith wrote a note of thanks to Marilyn, hinting she knew about the romance with Bobby and that he should bring her East sometime. The letter was found after Marilyn's death, but Mrs. Smith said she did not recall writing it. The timing, however, seems to jibe with other events involving Bobby.

Guests at Lawford's parties in 1961 and 1962 said there was

a familiarity between Marilyn and the Kennedy brothers that led them to believe she was involved with both Jack and Bobby. The wife of a well-known singer said, "It was rather obvious that Marilyn was very close to Bobby and Jack. One doesn't look for these things, but they didn't try to hide their feelings."

In early 1962, 20th Century-Fox offered Marilyn *Something's Got to Give*, a remake of *My Favorite Wife* (1940), with Irene Dunne, Cary Grant and Randolph Scott. Marilyn's part was a wife who was lost at sea and presumed dead. She comes home on her husband's wedding day.

Marilyn wasn't thrilled with the script, but she owed the studio two more films, and was anxious to fulfill her obligations. "Then I can name my own price like Elizabeth Taylor," she exclaimed.

Emotionally Marilyn was hanging on by a thread. Desperately wanting to believe in and trust people, she found it increasingly difficult after her divorce from Arthur Miller and the Yves Montand disaster. She truly believed Frank Sinatra would marry her, but he chose Juliet Prowse. Their engagement was brief, but Marilyn had been hurt deeply, though she and Frank remained friends.

In February of 1962, Marilyn got word that Arthur Miller was getting married. She also heard from a New York friend that his bride, Inge Morath, was pregnant. (The baby was born seven months after the wedding.) Even if Marilyn knew of her former husband's affair with the lady-photographer, his marriage had come as a shock. And the baby she so desperately wanted to give Arthur would come from Inge. Marilyn went into another deep depression, feeling more alone than ever before.

When she failed to show up at the studio for costume fittings, producer Henry Weinstein, a good friend of Dr. Greenson's, phoned and was disturbed by her weak voice and confused state of mind. He rushed to Marilyn's Brentwood home and found her in a barbiturate coma. Weinstein called a doctor and Marilyn's stomach was pumped once again.

At Dr. Greenson's suggestion, the studio allowed Marilyn to take a vacation. She visited Joe DiMaggio in Florida and then flew to Mexico where she shopped for furniture and knickknacks, but her depression lingered. Newsmen did not report Marilyn's heavy drinking and aimless dates with men. She was romanced by a young Mexican scriptwriter, José Bolanos, who followed her back to Los Angeles. At the Golden Globe event, he came over to Marilyn's table and sat down. She was annoyed, but tipsy enough to laugh it off. A photo taken of them that night made it appear as if Marilyn had a new romance. Bolanos got his fair share of publicity, and Marilyn got her share of bothersome phone calls from him.

In a fog, she spent three days with John Kennedy in Palm Springs and returned home to *Something's Got to Give*. Marilyn looked forward to working with Dean Martin, another member of Sinatra's Rat Pack, and George Cukor, who directed *Let's Make Love*.

But Marilyn had picked up a virus in Mexico that left her weak and short-tempered. She tore up revisions of the original script, written by her friend (and lover) Nunnally Johnson, had a blonde extra fired simply because the girl's hair color matched her own, and refused to work with Martin when he had a head cold. Marilyn insisted Henry Weinstein tell co-star Cyd Charisse to stop padding her bras. When he said that she didn't, Marilyn threatened, "Then I'll pad mine, and you'll have to redo all my costumes!"

Marilyn stayed home in bed if she had a fever, but her reputation for absences overshadowed any physical ailments. She showed up for work twelve out of thirty-five days, putting George Cukor in a difficult position, having to shoot around her. Dean Martin was a patient fellow and recited his dialogue to an absentee Marilyn with ease. When she did show up for work, it was a pathetic sight to those on the Fox lot watching the Sex Goddess get out of her limousine at the gate and throw up from sheer terror.

George Cukor, referred to disparagingly as a "woman's director," was used to Hollywood prima donnas such as Greta Garbo, Joan Crawford, Norma Shearer and Vivien Leigh. But he had reached the end of his rope with Marilyn, and word got back to her that George disliked her intensely. Had she been Joan Crawford, Cukor would have been cursed out in front of the cast, crew and God. But Marilyn did not have Crawford's ego, gall or confidence. So the relationship between Marilyn and Cukor during *Something's Got to Give* was strained despite his attempts to demonstrate warmth and understanding.

Marilyn was seeing Dr. Greenson every day for several hours, relying on him completely. Though he was the one responsible for holding together the broken pieces of her life and getting her to the studio occasionally, Greenson was worn out from the constant pressure. On May 10, 1962, he left for Europe on a vacation and Marilyn had a relapse. Her virus was worse, she told Henry Weinstein, who assumed she would not be well enough to attend President Kennedy's birthday bash at Madison Square Garden.

But on Thursday May 17, a helicopter landed on the Fox lot just before the noon break, and Peter Lawford whisked Marilyn aboard. Even though she had permission from the studio, Cukor was furious as were other Fox officials. In reflection, Weinstein says the studio should have taken advantage of the publicity by sending press agents and photographers to cover their star singing "Happy Birthday" to the President of the United States. Instead, Fox began playing with the idea of replacing Marilyn.

Perhaps there would not have been a crisis if the filming of *Cleopatra* was not costing Fox millions of dollars over budget. Elizabeth Taylor had been seriously ill with pneumonia and the elaborate sets were moved from damp London to sunny Rome, where the weather would be more beneficial to her health. "She's making a million dollars," Marilyn exclaimed, "but she can get sick and I can't!"

Fox executives had to answer to stockholders for monies spent on *Cleopatra* that rose to over $30 million. Though small in comparison, the cost of *Something's Got to Give* was mounting to almost $2 million due to Marilyn's absences. Under the circumstances, she made enemies by flying off to New York when production was so far behind schedule. Yet, as Henry Weinstein pointed out thirty years later, maybe Fox should have backed her up all the way because Marilyn was fêting the President of the United States. But Fox knew that she was also fêting her married lover.

Marilyn was jubilant on her flight to New York. She had ordered a dress designed by Jean-Louis for this very special occasion, a flesh-colored gown covered with oversized rhinestones that had to be sewn on to her nude curves. She paid $5,000 for this second layer of skin—a creation the world would never forget.

On Saturday, 19 May,* John Kennedy came to Madison Square Garden without his wife. Jackie chose to go horseback riding in Virginia when she heard that Marilyn would be there. Bobby came with his wife and other members of the Kennedy family, but he went backstage first.

James Spada wrote, in his book *Peter Lawford: The Man Who Kept the Secrets*, that Bobby asked Marilyn's hairdresser to leave the dressing room and closed the door. Fifteen minutes later Bobby left and the hairdresser looked in on Marilyn, who said with a giggle, "Could you help me get myself back together?"

Waiting to go on stage, Marilyn was a nervous wreck and very tipsy. Lawford introduced her three times before she appeared and a crowd of over 20,000 Democrats cheered. When Peter took her ermine wrap, the crowd went wild. Marilyn sang "Happy Birthday" to the President of the United States and gave this traditional song new meaning, as Whitney Houston

* JFK's actual birthday was May 29.

did with our national anthem.

Then Jack walked onstage and told the audience, "I can now retire from politics after having 'Happy Birthday' sung to me in such a sweet, wholesome way."

Backstage Marilyn introduced Isadore Miller to the President. She dearly loved her ex-father-in-law, who was proud to meet Kennedy. Marilyn's fawning over Isadore was both amusing and touching because he was so much shorter and she was wearing a dress that left nothing to the imagination.

Later that same evening, Marilyn attended a private party in Jack's honor. Arthur Schlesinger, Jr., wrote in his journal that he and Bobby engaged in mock competition for Marilyn. Adlai Stevenson said he could only get to her "after breaking through the strong defenses by Robert Kennedy, who was dodging around her like a moth around the flame."

Those who knew about Marilyn's affair with the President were almost positive he had "given" her to Bobby, who wasn't known to be so obviously engaged by a woman. But around 2:00 A.M., John and Marilyn left separately and met at the Carlyle Hotel for two hours. This turned out to be the last time they would be together.

Bobby had been warned that Hoffa, Giancana and Hoover knew too much about Jack's sexual affairs. He had to be more careful. Everyone knew about Marilyn, and her public display at Madison Square Garden gave Jack's enemies exactly what they wanted, all wrapped up in a pretty rhinestone package. Jackie's absence was proof positive.

Letting Marilyn go didn't faze Jack, but someone had to tell her not to bother him anymore. Someone who could make her understand his political future was at stake as well as his marriage to Jackie. Someone who could explain to her that Catholic politicians can't get a divorce and expect to live in the White House. Someone who could approach this calmly and gently, but firmly.

That someone was Bobby Kennedy.

21

Someone Has to Give

Jack's sharing Marilyn with Bobby on the night of his birthday celebration did not surprise her. For a long time she had known about Lawford's "girlie" parties and that Jack participated. Marilyn probably knew about Peter's sexual hang-ups, also. But she wanted nothing to do with these orgies at the beach house.

Marilyn did not know, however, that May 19, 1962, after the Madison Square Garden bash, was to be her last night of intimacy with Jack, because she told friends they were getting together when he came to California during the summer. It would be Bobby's responsibility to make sure this did not happen.

Though she was exhausted from her trip to New York, Marilyn reported to the studio on Monday morning in a good mood and ready to work. On Tuesday she was scheduled for the "nude" swimming scene in which she tries to lure Dean Martin into the pool with her. When the cameraman said it was impossible to hide Marilyn's flesh-colored bathing suit, she took it off. The set was immediately closed to outsiders, but there were three photographers from the studio who were allowed to take all the pictures they wanted.

Marilyn gave permission to use the best of the lot provided

the magazines used her on the cover instead of Elizabeth Taylor, whose romance with Richard Burton on and off the set of *Cleopatra* dominated the periodicals.

Marilyn succeeded in replacing Miss Taylor on magazine covers around the world. Even before the semi-nude pictures were released, all the publicity generated by her filming a movie scene in the nude was colossal. This was unheard of in 1962. The photo of a carefree Marilyn in the water, her arm leaning on the edge of the pool and one leg propped up was tame, but the fact she wasn't wearing anything made it reek of sexuality. *Life*, *Vogue* and *Cosmopolitan* magazines arranged for interviews with Marilyn, and *Playboy*, which was relatively new, bought her most revealing nudes for an unparalleled $25,000.

It was an uplifting few weeks for Marilyn. She talked to Bobby on the telephone, but Jack refused to take or return her calls. Nor did he respond to her romantic and frequently embarrassing letters.

On Friday, June 1, Marilyn was thirty-six. The cast of *Something's Got to Give* surprised her with a birthday cake, but there was a feeling of forced gaiety on everyone's part. Unbeknownst to Marilyn, Weinstein and Cukor were dismayed by her appearance on film. Watching the rushes every night, they saw a beautiful star going through the motions and little else. Marilyn wasn't radiating her character's moods or feelings. She was hazy, wooden and disconnected on film.

But on the night of her birthday, Marilyn was anything but hazy and wooden when she appeared for a Muscular-Dystrophy benefit at Dodger Stadium. Wearing a baseball cap, she joked with the players and posed for pictures before throwing out the first ball. This was the last public appearance she would make.

Hollywood columnist Sheila Graham wrote that Marilyn had celebrated her birthday with Frank Sinatra at Trader Vic's in Beverly Hills. There was no mention of the fact that she was very, very drunk.

On the weekend following her birthday, Marilyn went into a

deep state of depression. The psychiatrist who was subbing for Dr. Greenson in his absence was appalled to see pill bottles scattered around her bedroom and threw them away.

On Monday morning Marilyn did not report for work. The excuse was her lingering virus. Weinstein was furious. He had asked her not to stand around in the cold air at Dodger Stadium. Unfortunately, it was not a simple virus that plagued Marilyn. Something or someone triggered her collapse. Without pills, it was possible she was going through withdrawal. Or did Marilyn find out she was pregnant again and struggling with herself for a solution?

Dr. Greenson, vacationing in Europe, telephoned Henry Weinstein that he was flying back to California immediately, assuring him everything would be all right. But he was too late. On Wednesday, June 6, the *New York Mirror*'s front-page headline read MARILYN BOUNCED!

It wasn't official until Friday, June 8, when Marilyn went to the studio and was told to her face that she was finished. Bob Slatzer said, "She was crying on the phone, but I think Marilyn was in shock more than anything. Then she got angry and said she was going to do something constructive about it. Fox sued Marilyn and she sued them back. When Dean Martin refused to work without her, Fox sued him and he countersued. Martin held all the aces, however, because his contract gave him the right of approval over his co-star. He made it clear. No Monroe? No Martin!"

Lee Remick, who signed a contract with Fox to do *Something's Got to Give*, said, "I feel Marilyn should have been replaced. I don't believe actors should be allowed to get away with that type of behavior." On June 20, Remick's contract was cancelled and Marilyn was reinstated at a salary more than double what it was originally. The money was important, but she was just as proud that Dean Martin had come to her defense. Fox announced they would resume filming in September after Martin returned from his nightclub tour.

Marilyn was overheard chatting with someone about the summer months ahead. "Your skin is so white, Marilyn. What you need is a tan."

"Yeah," she sighed. "A tan *and* a man."

On June 26, Bobby Kennedy had dinner with Marilyn at the beach house and spent the night. We have to suppose they discussed the President's lack of response to her calls and letters. Getting through to Marilyn was difficult for Bobby. She was unable to fathom Jack's coldness and lack of interest in maintaining a friendship, if nothing more. Marilyn was at her most vulnerable—a sensitive lost child who could not fall back on her acting to camouflage the disappointment of being abandoned again.

Bobby was not immune to her pain. His sympathy for Marilyn prevented him from being objective though he got the message across that her affair with his brother was over. Had he not been attracted to Marilyn and on the verge of falling in love with her, if he wasn't already, Bobby could have prevented the heartbreaks that followed. Instead of laying down the law and getting back to politics, he got deeply and emotionally involved with her.

Marilyn told close friends she wasn't physically attracted to Bobby initially. That his intellect intrigued her was typical of Marilyn à la Fred Karger, Bob Slatzer and Arthur Miller. She forgot about being the First Lady and permitted herself to get caught up in dreams of marrying the Attorney General of the United States. How much Bobby contributed to this fantasy isn't known, but he was guilty of allowing her to believe it.

On Friday, June 27, Marilyn's neighbors saw Bobby drive up to her Brentwood home in a Cadillac convertible with the top down. In this regard, he was far more reckless than his brother. Peter Lawford's neighbors recalled seeing Bobby getting out of his car often and Marilyn arriving soon after. Quite openly they were seen together talking alone on the terrace or strolling the beach. Lawford's neighbor and good friend Peter Dye said,

"She was crazy about him. She told me. I think he was nuts about her, too."

Marilyn wasn't forewarned about Jack because it was common knowledge he was a womanizer. But friends, including Pat and Peter Lawford, hinted she had no future with Bobby, either. The affair was very, very delicate at this time because Marilyn knew she was pregnant. Most likely she confided in the Lawfords because they covered for her when she had the abortion. Though Marilyn had dated Frank Sinatra, José Bolanos and other men in the past few months, the father was undoubtedly Jack or Bobby Kennedy. Her pregnancy was cause for alarm, needless to say, and it was Bobby who had to see it through to the end. Marilyn called him regularly as her telephone records indicate. Bobby's secretary said he returned her calls even if he was in conference.

Marilyn was able to get through to him until Monday, July 23. This is significant because she had had an abortion at Cedars of Lebanon Hospital on the previous Friday. A select few knew the truth. The others were told Marilyn was at Lake Tahoe with the Lawfords. Why she would bother mentioning to several acquaintances that she had suffered a recent miscarriage is a mystery.

After Marilyn's call to Bobby at the Justice Department on Monday, he had his private number changed and the switchboard would not give her any information. Obviously, Bobby wanted to make sure Marilyn had not changed her mind about the abortion. One can only imagine what she was going through. It's doubtful Marilyn would have had the baby, but being told to get rid of it and then being dumped like so much garbage by another Kennedy was pathetic.

Knowing Bob Slatzer was going out of town the last week in July, Marilyn called him from a phone booth. She'd been doing that a lot lately "because I hear clicking sounds on my telephone." Bob picked her up and drove to a beach in Point Dume. He saw more than the normal signs of aging in

Marilyn's face. Her smile seemed forced at times, unusual for a woman who liked to laugh so much. He could tell that something was really bothering her. Then she handed him a small book with a red cover.

"What is it?" Slatzer asked when she handed it to him.

"It's my diary. I want you to look through it."

"What's this scribbling about Murder, Inc.?" he asked.

"Bobby told me he was powerful enough to have people taken care of if they got in his way."

Slatzer was stunned by the contents of the little red book. "Do you know what the Bay of Pigs was?" he asked her.

"I think that was down in Cuba," she answered. "Bobby said he handled the whole thing because Jack had taken medication for his back and wasn't feeling well. That's why I'm so frightened and confused. He has all those gangster connections, and he told me stuff about Mr. Hoffa. I just don't know how it's all going to turn out. Bobby promised to marry me. But will he? He's been ignoring me. I've tried to reach him by phone and I just can't get to him. What does it mean?"

"It means," Slatzer said bluntly, "that he doesn't want anything more to do with you. And for your own good, you'd better forget him."

"Would he lie to me?" she asked. "About marrying me?"

"I think so, Marilyn."

"Maybe his wife would like to know some of the things he told me. It's all here. I'm glad I made these notes."

"Have you shown the diary to anyone else?" Slatzer asked.

"Nobody. Bobby saw it once and told me to get rid of it."

Slatzer asked her to do the same thing. "What you have here is very dangerous. If you don't burn it, put the damn thing in a vault."

On the drive home Marilyn said out of the blue, "Bobby meant what he said or he'd never have made those promises to me. He told me I would have to wait until he got a few things straightened out."

"Forget him," Slatzer repeated.

"I can't do that," she spoke up. "He owes me an explanation."

Marilyn spent the last weekend of July with the Lawfords in Lake Tahoe at the Cal-Neva Lodge, owned by Sam Giancana and Frank Sinatra. Marilyn appeared to be drunk, drugged or both. Peter apparently encouraged her to drink and take pills. Though reliable sources claim his motive was getting Marilyn to participate in orgies, it seems unlikely since Pat Lawford was there. For sure, Peter wanted to loosen her tongue and he succeeded. Marilyn told him she was planning to "tell all" about her affairs with the Kennedy brothers because her telephone messages were ignored. She had gone so far as to call Bobby's home. "I'm tired of being used," Marilyn said. "I'm going public with everything."

Despite her oblivion, Marilyn had the sense to leave the phone off the hook when she went to bed. The switchboard operator, disturbed by Marilyn's heavy breathing and then a thud, called Pat and Peter who found her on the floor. They managed to keep Marilyn on her feet until she came around. Sinatra heard about it and was thoroughly disgusted. But Lawford was more concerned about Marilyn's plans for revenge.

Pat flew to the East Coast, and Peter accompanied Marilyn back to Los Angeles in Sinatra's private plane. Observers said they were both drunk and unkempt.

Anthony Summers reported that Lawford stopped at a pay phone not far from home and talked for thirty minutes. Apparently he had been alerted that his beach house was bugged and the phones were tapped. It must have been a very important call if he kept others in the limousine waiting for that length of time. We can only guess that Peter was talking to Bobby about Marilyn's threats and the possibility that Hoffa already had damaging tapes in his possession.

Author James Spada stated in his biography of Peter Lawford that Bobby found out Marilyn had wiretapped her own house to get evidence of their relationship. In doing so, she had sealed her own fate.

In the middle of this intrigue was Hollywood detective Fred Otash, who arranged the wiretappings for Jimmy Hoffa. Peter and Marilyn did not know Otash was involved, and approached him separately from their own recording devices.

DiMaggio wanted to buy Hoffa's tapes to save Marilyn from another nervous collapse. On one of his last visits to her home, they argued over Bobby, and Joe stormed out in a rage. Three years after her death, Robert Kennedy was at Yankee Stadium to honor baseball hero Mickey Mantle. Bobby shook hands with the former Yankees who were lined up on the field, but DiMaggio stepped back when Kennedy approached.

Though Marilyn's career was more promising than ever, her obsession with Bobby took precedence over everything else the last week of her life. She trusted only Dr. Greenson and a few close friends. Marilyn spent a good deal of time with Lawford, who tried to convince her that Bobby was under enormous pressure. Peter said he was told by someone involved in the wire-tappings, that phones in the Justice Department were bugged, also.

But Marilyn was interested only in talking to Bobby and finding out why he had walked out of her life without an explanation.

Bob Slatzer was in Ohio on business that week. "I spoke to Marilyn every day," he said. "She hoped to do a movie with Frank Sinatra and a film about Jean Harlow. She turned down an offer to do a stage show in Las Vegas because she wanted to concentrate on her film career. Marilyn was bubbling about a lot of good things that were happening. She was having work done on the house and doing her own gardening. Then—and I'd been expecting it—she brought up Bobby Kennedy. Marilyn couldn't close this chapter of her life until she got in touch with him."

Marilyn used to drink Bloody Marys first thing in the morning. Now it was champagne and pills for breakfast. After her death, Dr. Greenson said Marilyn belonged in a sanitarium, but he knew this would destroy her. Over the years, friends have commented about Marilyn's behavior and appearance during this critical time. Some say she looked beautiful and had a positive attitude, but the majority were saddened to see her wilting before their eyes. Some people said they saw a Marilyn Monroe who didn't give a damn anymore. Her slacks were often torn and stained, and her hair, skin and eyes were lifeless. The glow had disappeared. A repairman, working on her house, said, "She looked terrible. Just awful. She reminded me of an unfinished portrait. The beauty was there without the color."

On Thursday, August 2, 1962, Bob Slatzer called Marilyn about Bobby Kennedy's plans to spend the weekend in San Francisco. "She perked up," Slatzer said. Marilyn's obsession with asking Dr. Greenson for advice prompted her to make a second appointment with him that day. Later, Marilyn had dinner with Lawford at the beach house.

The next day she tried to reach Kennedy in Washington, but couldn't get through to him or find out where he would be staying in San Francisco. She called Slatzer from a pay phone. "Are you *sure* he's going to be out here, Bob?"

"According to my information he should be on his way as we speak," he said.

"If he keeps avoiding me, I might just call a press conference."

"That's the worst thing you could do!"

"If he's out here, I'll get in touch with him," she persisted.

Bob knew it was a lost cause trying to change her mind. They discussed Marilyn's trip to New York in about ten days. "I'll stop off in Columbus to see you on my way back," she said.

This would be her last conversation with Bob Slatzer.

Marilyn called Hyannis Port and spoke to Pat Lawford, who said that Bobby, his wife Ethel and their four children had reservations at the St. Francis Hotel in San Francisco. Marilyn left several messages for Bobby, who did not return the calls. Did he bring his family as an excuse not to see her?

There are several versions as to where Marilyn was on Friday night, August 3, such as her flying to San Francisco to find Bobby.

Jean Leon, proprietor of the elegant La Scala restaurant, claims Marilyn ordered food and he delivered it personally to her home. Leon said someone else was with her that night, someone he refused to identify.

Another source has Marilyn at La Scala having dinner with Bobby Kennedy.

The believable version was related to Slatzer by Monroe's press aide Pat Newcomb, who had dinner with Marilyn at Frascati restaurant in Beverly Hills. Peter and a friend joined them. Marilyn's former dress designer (and lover), Billy Travilla was dining at the same restaurant. He hadn't seen her in a while and went over to her table. "I couldn't believe it was the same Marilyn," he said. "It was a different girl. She looked at me as if she didn't know who the hell I was. I was embarrassed. Then she said, 'Billy!' and introduced me. I was going to jot her a note and tell her off, but I would never have forgiven myself because the next day she was dead."

Marilyn had a sleepless night. She told Jeanne Carmen that a woman kept calling and repeating, "Leave Bobby alone, you tramp! Leave Bobby alone!" Marilyn said the voice was familiar, but she couldn't place it. Exhausted and lonely, she asked Jeanne to come over "with a bag of sleeping pills and we'll drink some wine." Carmen said she was busy all day, but would call back later.

What happened during the afternoon and evening hours of August 4, 1962, hasn't been firmly established. For a long time the pieces to this puzzle were missing. Marilyn's housekeeper Mrs. Murray stuck to her well-rehearsed story for twenty-three years: at 8 P.M., after an uneventful day, Marilyn went to bed. Around 3 A.M., Mrs. Murray woke up and noticed a light under Marilyn's locked door. When she knocked and got no response, she went outside, looked in the window and saw Marilyn lying rigid on the bed with the phone clutched in her hand. Mrs. Murray immediately called Dr. Greenson who arrived five minutes later, broke the bedroom window and entered. He could see Marilyn was no longer living and called her personal physician Dr. Hyman Engelberg. The police were notified at 4:25 A.M.

Mrs. Murray departed from this story off-and-on until she finally got down to the nitty-gritty in 1985. She said on August 4, Bobby Kennedy came to see Marilyn, who became hysterical during a violent argument and "his protectors had to step in."

Mrs. Murray also admitted that Marilyn was *not* dead when the doctor arrived. A Schaefer ambulance was summoned. Marilyn was comatose and rushed to Santa Monica Hospital, where she died. Ambulance Service owner Walt Schaefer had no idea who returned the body to her house because he wasn't working that night. The ambulance driver, who supposedly took Marilyn to the hospital, denied he was on duty at that time and told author-investigator Anthony Summers, "Don't bother calling me anymore!"

Walt Schaefer told Bob Slatzer in 1985 that a bill for his ambulance service was paid by the Monroe estate. These records disappeared out of her Probate file. However, Marilyn's neighbors told Slatzer they saw a Schaefer ambulance parked in front of her house on the night she died.

Schaefer said he did not volunteer this information because over 80 percent of his business came from city and county sources who wanted the truth "swept under the carpet."

22

Cursum Perficio

Coroner Dr. Thomas Noguchi concluded that Marilyn Monroe's death was a "probable suicide" caused by acute barbiturate poisoning due to ingestion of overdose.

Even before the funeral, however, contradictory evidence began to surface. Joe Hyams, correspondent for the *New York Herald-Tribune*, rushed to 12305 Fifth Helena Drive on the morning of August 5, 1962. As he walked toward the house Hyams saw a wheeled stretcher. On top of it, under a pink blanket, a body was anchored down with leather straps at the feet and across the chest. An old battered Ford panel truck came up the street and stopped by the stretcher. He watched as a man trundled the body onto the back of the truck.

Hyams introduced himself to one of the neighbors—an elderly woman in a housecoat and slippers, and asked her what he considered to be a routine question: "Did you hear anything odd last night?"

"Nothing out of the ordinary," she replied. "Just that damn helicopter buzzing the house."

At the time Hyams thought nothing of it. Marilyn had supposedly died with a telephone receiver near her hand, and he was more interested in finding out who she called. The following day Hyams contacted a telephone company employee for a copy of the numbers on Marilyn's tape, but was told this information had been impounded by the FBI.

"Is that customary?" Hyams asked in disbelief.

"Hell, no," was the reply. "I've never before heard of the government getting in on the act. Obviously somebody high up ordered it."

Hyams had heard rumors about Marilyn's affair with the President of the United States. If anyone had the power to seize telephone records, it was John Kennedy. Hyams and a colleague gained access to the log of helicopter rentals at nearby Culver Field and discovered that a chopper flew someone from Lawford's beach house to Los Angeles airport around 2 A.M. on Sunday, August 5.

Bobby Kennedy was seen at the Beverly Hilton Hotel on Saturday by several people, including Police Chief William Parker. Neighbors saw Bobby at Lawford's place and going into Marilyn's house. Whatever happened in the course of the afternoon and evening of August 4, Bobby apparently made a fast exit back to San Francisco early Sunday morning.

Bob Slatzer returned to Hollywood on Monday and spoke to Marilyn's business manager, Inez Melson. "She thought I might like to have a memento or something and suggested we meet at Marilyn's place," Bob said. "I took a walk around the grounds and accidentally came across some broken glass *outside* the bedroom window. If Dr. Greenson had broken the pane to gain access, the shattered pieces should have been on the *inside*. I knew then that those involved were lying, and I began my investigation to prove that Marilyn did not take her own life."

Ten years after her death, Slatzer's book *The Life and Curious Death of Marilyn Monroe* was halted by life-threatening phone calls. "Slatzer, if the Monroe book comes out," the voice said, "you'll be killed. There will be a contract out for you."

"Is there one now?" Slatzer asked.

"You better believe it. You better believe it."

Bob called the police after his editor's friend was beaten into unconsciousness. "We're going to give Slatzer the same thing," one of the thugs said. As a result, the police provided Bob with the necessary protection.

Slatzer's book went into print two years later without incident. More than royalties, he wanted an inquest that was not forthcoming. "They found no trace of barbiturates in Marilyn's stomach or digestive tract," Slatzer said. "The small intestine, which would contain undissolved sleeping capsules, wasn't checked. The barbiturate level in Marilyn's bloodstream was 4.5 milligrams percent. Yet no trace of drugs in any of the organs was indicated. Marilyn's autopsy report was conveniently "lost," and her organ specimens disappeared.

"The plumbing in her bathroom was being fixed so she had no water to swallow forty-seven Nembutal pills, as her doctors claimed. Marilyn couldn't swallow an aspirin without water. There wasn't even a drinking glass in her room."

Sergeant Jack Clemmons of the Central Los Angeles police department was the first to arrive at Marilyn's. He saw right away she had postmortem lividity and that the body had been moved or "rearranged." Dr. Engleberg appeared to be genuinely grieved, but Dr. Greenson had a nervous smirk on his face that disturbed Clemmons, and Mrs. Murray was doing the laundry at 5 A.M.!

Slatzer's attempt to publish his book in 1972 was mentioned in the *Los Angeles Herald-Examiner*. As a result, he received a call from a man who identified himself as Jack Quinn. Bob doubted it was his real name, but the man was able to establish his credibility. Quinn claimed the original report on the investigation of Marilyn's death amounted to 723 pages that dwindled down to only 54.

"She had bruises on her, but they were edited out of the final report," Quinn said.

"What bruises?" Bob asked.

"Under the armpit."

The most startling bit of intelligence that Quinn imparted to Bob was statements made by Bobby Kennedy to the Los Angeles Police Department.

"Did you know she was bugging JFK?"

Slatzer was stunned. "John F!"

"Yeah, that's right. From what I saw in the deposition, it said there was a divorce pending with Jackie and JFK."

"Wasn't anything said about Bobby's having an affair with Marilyn?" Slatzer asked.

"No. Bobby said the President dispatched him to come out here and talk to Marilyn because JFK was getting a lot of phone calls from her. Bobby said he and Peter Lawford went to Marilyn's house late in the afternoon on August 4. There was a violent argument. She lunged at Bobby and clawed at him. He grabbed Marilyn and threw her to the floor. Then she was given an injection of pentobarbital in her armpit, which settled her down."

"Did Bobby or Peter give Marilyn the injection?"

"No. One of them called for a doctor to come over."

This made sense to Slatzer because one of Marilyn's neighbors had a card party that afternoon and the ladies told Bob they saw the Attorney General arrive with a man carrying a physician's bag. Slatzer theorized Kennedy slipped out of the house and returned with a doctor.

Quinn said Marilyn was given a shot of pentobarbital under her left arm, adding, "RFK even named the artery on the tape. I can't remember the doctor's name, but it's also on record that Dr. Greenson came to Marilyn's house at five-thirty that day and gave her a shot, but he didn't name the drug."

(Dr. Noguchi said he went over every inch of Marilyn's body with a magnifying glass and found no needle marks. Yet, she apparently received two injections just prior to her death.)

The revelations of Jack Quinn to Slatzer in 1972 are almost identical to new evidence uncovered by Anthony Summers in

1991 that involves a recording of the bitter argument Marilyn had with Bobby Kennedy on August 4, 1962. (The tape belonged to Bernie Spindel, who was Jimmy Hoffa's personal "wireman.")

Peter Lawford was also there and trying to referee. Bobby demanded to know where the recording device was hidden and, in turn, was willing to work something out with Marilyn, who was only interested in why Bobby had changed his mind about marrying her. There was a good deal of screaming and then loud thuds that sounded like a brutal physical fight. (Summers' source did not know everything that was on this explosive tape.)

Marilyn was invited to dinner that night at Peter Lawford's, where she had planned to meet Bobby. After the vicious argument, she knew their affair was over for good. Around 5 P.M., a drugged and depressed Marilyn called Dr. Greenson, who came to the house and stayed with her until 7:15. Shortly thereafter, Marilyn called Peter to tell him not to expect her for dinner. During the course of the evening she spoke to a number of friends.

Around 9:30 P.M. Marilyn called Jeanne Carmen again.

"Please, Jeanne, please come over."

"I can't, Marilyn."

"Could you bring me some sleeping pills?"

"I can't come over tonight, Marilyn. I just can't."

Carmen related their last conversation in tears, but said in a television interview recently, "Maybe I could have saved her ... nothing would have happened, but Marilyn was going to talk to the press on Monday, and people might have been desperate and wanted to get rid of her."

Most likely, Marilyn's last call was to Lawford around 10:00. "Say good-bye to Pat," she mumbled, "say good-bye to Jack, and say good-bye to yourself because you're a nice guy." Peter said she didn't hang up the phone. There was only silence. He tried calling her back several times, but the line was busy. Lawford had been through other episodes with Marilyn and made a remark to one of his dinner guests, "It's phone-dangling time again." Remembering what happened at Cal-Neva Lodge, he tried calling Marilyn again to no avail and decided to go to her house a good hour after their phone conversation. Since Peter was not man enough to go alone, somebody or somebodies went with him. If what he told Otash was true, Bobby Kennedy was with Lawford when they found Marilyn in a coma. A Schaefer ambulance rushed her to Santa Monica Hospital, where she died. Who got her back home and into her own bed remains a mystery, but only someone with power and influence could accomplish such a feat as well as having Marilyn's telephone records seized within hours.

If Bobby was picked up around 2:00 A.M. at Lawford's beach house, it's possible that Dr. Greenson did not get a call until 3:30 A.M.

Much of the confusion can be blamed on Peter Lawford's lying to protect the Kennedys, and then changing his stories so often over the years until his death in 1984. But Lawford was not lying to investigator Fred Otash at 3 A.M. on August 5. "Peter was in a state of shock," Otash said. "He told me that Marilyn Monroe was dead … Bobby Kennedy had been there and was spirited out of town by plane. Lawford wanted me to go to Marilyn's house and pick up any or all informations that linked her to the Kennedys."

Otash did not want to get involved, but contacted someone else who arrived at Marilyn's house too late for any snooping around. There was nothing of a personal nature, anyway. Her file cabinet had been broken into. Whatever she locked up for safekeeping was missing.

Lawford told his third wife, Deborah Gould, that he had straightened up Marilyn's house and destroyed a suicide note.

He did not tell Deborah what it said.

Marilyn's half-sister Berneice Miracle asked Joe DiMaggio to claim the body and make funeral arrangements. While Arthur Miller said, "I'm sorry, but it was inevitable," an inconsolable DiMaggio blamed Frank Sinatra and the Kennedys for Marilyn's death. He did not want the stench of Hollywood in the Westwood Memorial Park Chapel. Nor allow them to look upon his goddess wearing a green Pucci dress, lying on a bed of champagne velvet in a bronze casket, her hands clasping a tiny bouquet of roses from him.

Joe spent the night before the funeral alone with Marilyn. Less than thirty people were allowed in the chapel, among them the Greensons and the Strasbergs. The other mourners had worked for Marilyn in some capacity.

Pat Lawford flew in from Hyannis Port, but she and Peter were not allowed in the chapel. Frank Sinatra tried to force his way in with Sammy Davis, Jr., but they were firmly turned away. Many of Marilyn's co-stars planned to attend, but a spokesman for the mortuary on Wednesday, August 8, announced that only those closest to Miss Monroe had been invited. "No movie stars will be present. Mr. DiMaggio is making all the decisions. No one will view the remains."

After Lee Strasberg's brief eulogy and a few words from a pastor, the service ended with a rendition of "Over the Rainbow." Then the coffin was opened and Joe DiMaggio sobbed, "I love you," and kissed Marilyn one last time.

A black Cadillac hearse drove the short distance to the Corridor of Memories, where the casket was sealed in a crypt. Against a piece of rose marble is a bronze plaque that reads ...

MARILYN MONROE

1926–1962

Joe DiMaggio had a pair of red roses delivered to the crypt three times a week. In 1982 Bob Slatzer noticed there were no flowers on Marilyn's crypt, and arranged to have them sent on his behalf.

23

A Tragic Mistake or Murder?

When Elizabeth Taylor heard about Marilyn's death, she told the press, "I can't believe it was suicide. I think she accidentally overdosed on sleeping pills." Elizabeth confided in friends, "I was stunned about Marilyn. I thought it would have been me."

Some years later, Elizabeth tore into columnist Max Lerner about a magazine article he'd written about her entitled ELIZABETH TAYLOR: SURVIVOR. Lerner said, "She called me in a rage. I had written that she was a legend but that Marilyn Monroe was a myth—perhaps *the* American myth of a love goddess—and Elizabeth really let me have it. 'You goddamned son-of-a-bitch!' she screamed. 'You have the nerve saying that Marilyn was a myth and I'm a lousy legend? I'm much more beautiful than Marilyn Monroe ever was, and I'm certainly a much better actress. What the hell do I have to do to be a myth? Die young and at my own hand!' "

Darryl Zanuck, president of 20th Century-Fox, said "Nobody discovered her [Marilyn]. She earned her way to stardom."

There should have been a statement from the White House, as is often the case when a popular celebrity dies, especially one as friendly with the Kennedys as Marilyn, who sang "Happy Birthday" to the President on national television. But the only comment came from Jackie Kennedy who told reporters, "She will go on eternally."

Sir Laurence Olivier said, "Miss Monroe was exploited beyond anyone's means."

Frank Sinatra was devastated. "I'll miss her very much," he said with tears in his eyes.

Joshua Logan thought Marilyn was "one of the most unappreciated people in the world."

Billy Wilder's opinion of Marilyn softened a bit but remained consistent: "She had flesh impact which is rare. Clara Bow had it. So did Jean Harlow. It was worth a week's torment to get three luminous minutes on the screen."

John Huston said it was apparent during *The Misfits* that Marilyn was a troubled woman. "I knew in a few years she would either be dead or institutionalized."

Joseph Mankiewicz, who directed Marilyn in *All About Eve*, was blunt—"She died at the right time. She was old, fat and unloved." Most likely Mankiewicz hadn't seen Marilyn in a while because she was slim and beautiful in film clips of *Something's Got to Give*.

Peter Lawford blamed himself for Marilyn's death. Had he responded an hour sooner, she might have survived. Based on what he told Fred Otash in a panic, Bobby Kennedy was also in the rescue party and taking a big risk. The ambulance drivers and emergency room attendants at Santa Monica Hospital could easily have verified the Attorney General's presence. Hospital records have long since been destroyed, but those involved in trying to revive Marilyn have never come forth. It's possible they didn't recognize her, but most logically the cover-up came all the way from Washington after Peter's call to Jack that night. If Bobby tried to save Marilyn, it would lend a touch of warmth and caring to the hard and cold facts of her death.

Dr. Greenson could not divulge what he knew about Marilyn

and the Kennedys, but he had a lengthy session with a Deputy District Attorney, John Miner, who related, "We discussed the death of his patient, Marilyn Monroe, for several hours. As a result of what Dr. Greenson told me, and from what I heard on tape recordings, I believe I can say definitely it was not suicide."

Two years after Marilyn died, Greenson hurriedly told a reporter over the phone, "I can't explain or defend myself without revealing things that I don't want to reveal ... I feel I can't draw a line and say I'll tell you this, but I won't tell you that. . . . It's a terrible position to be in, to have to say I can't talk about it because I can't tell the whole story. Listen ... talk to Bobby Kennedy."

But former Sergeant Jack Clemmons told British author Sandra Shevey that Marilyn's psychiatrist might not have been blameless: "Greenson never admitted what we know to be true, on account of the Kennedy deposition, to having injected Monroe—even accidentally. Why didn't he admit it? Why, if it was an accident? Why the lies?"

In 1979, a former coroner's aide, Lionel Grandison, made a public statement that he had been reluctant to sign Marilyn's death certificate, but his superiors forced him to do so. Grandison said the investigation was a farce.

Bob Slatzer brings to light more activity on the night Marilyn died. "The procedure in Hollywood was that studio officials were summoned before anyone else if their contract players were involved in misconduct, murder, suicide, drunk driving and so forth," he said. "This gives the studios a chance to avoid scandal or leakage to the press about their stars. Knowing this, I checked into it and was told that Fox VIPs and Kennedy's entourage were at Marilyn's before the police arrived."

Marilyn, who believed in life after death, might have been amused to see a gathering of such distinguished people in her little house. But when they removed her body, she lay unclaimed in the morgue with a tag on her big toe marked Case

No. 81128 ... back where she came from as the rejected Norma Jeane, an unwanted burden, an abused and lonely child.

Her body was finally claimed by Inez Melson and prepared for burial. Some years before, Marilyn told Whitey Snyder, "If anything happens to me, promise you'll make me up." Shaken by her death, he took a bottle of gin to the mortuary. Snyder, costumier Margie Plecher and hairdresser Agnes Flanagan worked diligently on Marilyn as if she were about to face the camera.

In Whitey's pocket was a money clip from Marilyn with the inscription, "While I'm still warm. ..."

Bobby Kennedy was attending church with his family in San Francisco when news of Marilyn's death was broadcast. Their host for the weekend, attorney John Bates, denied that the Attorney General was in Los Angeles. Interviewed by BBC in 1985, Bates stuck to his story, and said there was little reaction, if any, when reports of Marilyn's death came over the car radio.

Bobby then took his family on a camping trip and to the World's Fair in Seattle. One can only speculate his mixed emotions ranging from disgust and relief to sadness. But for Bobby, the scandal still loomed. He knew Jimmy Hoffa had tapes that could ruin him—tapes that were not for sale to the Kennedys. At election time, the Republicans might be interested if the price was right.

No, Marilyn's death had not saved Bobby's political reputation. It's doubtful she would have gone through with the press conference, anyway. Marilyn was not vindictive. She was a passionate woman in love with a man who promised to marry her. The Spindel tape proved that. Bobby said he'd make any arrangements she wanted, but Marilyn obviously ignored the financial offer for a simple explanation as to why she could never see or talk to the Kennedys again.

There was a rebound theory, too. A month or so before she died, Marilyn told her close friend, columnist Sidney Skolsky, that she couldn't forget Jack. "I can't get him out of my mind," she said. Skolsky was stunned and did not pursue the subject.

The answer is obvious, but not so simple. The President never hinted at marriage, but the Attorney General did. If one really wants to stretch the imagination, Marilyn could have had her private moments with Jack if she'd married his younger brother. She had learned to play their game. . . .

Marilyn's notebook or so-called diary has been emphasized over the years. On a recent television documentary the narrator said, "Marilyn was no dumb blonde," referring to the information she had jotted down. This made her a security risk because one doesn't go around with written proof: "Bobby told me the CIA had a deal with the Mafia to kill Castro. In return, the mob would regain control of the Havana casinos."

Slatzer said Marilyn was frightened because her phone was bugged, but she ignored his warnings about the diary. To Marilyn it was a notebook she kept "for the love of Bobby." Anything to impress him, anything to prove she was a good listener and well informed. Jimmy Hoffa and J. Edgar Hoover were not interested in Marilyn's diary. They had recorded what she had scribbled.

In 1972 Slatzer consulted Milo Spiriglio, director-in-chief of Nick Harris Detectives, Inc., the second-oldest detective agency in the nation. "The possibility that Marilyn Monroe was murdered to forever seal her lips greatly outweighs the theory of taking her own life," Spiriglio said in support of Slatzer's investigation. "We the people are entitled to know the truth, and once and for all end this political cover-up. Homicide has no statute of limitations. The death of Marilyn Monroe needs to be reopened in the courtroom. Only then can the case be closed to the satisfaction of the public."

Spiriglio, retained by Slatzer to assist in his investigation, was contacted by three Mafia members who said that Sam Giancana ordered the murder of Marilyn, either "to protect or to embarrass the Kennedys." Spiriglio got approval from the Mafia to reveal this much and nothing more "yet." He claims that Marilyn's death was not caused by pills or an injection.

Author-journalist John Austin agrees with this theory, but thinks Marilyn was sedated by someone she knew. In his recent book *Hollywood's Unsolved Mysteries*, Austin emphasizes that Marilyn's autopsy showed some discoloration of the colon: "It must indicate that it [Nembutal] was administered in the area by suppository or by enema, possibly by someone she trusted. In this case, it was probably Dr. Greenson."

Another cause of death emerged recently. Two very close friends of Marilyn's who wish to remain anonymous believe that Robert Kennedy accidentally smothered her with a pillow during their violent fight on August 4. Unconscious, Marilyn died in the ambulance and was taken back home where her body was laid out on the bed to make it appear as if she committed suicide.

Any and all theories are worth mentioning because Marilyn Monroe was a fairy tale heroine who did not live happily ever after. . . .

24

What Goes Around, Comes Around

On August 7, 1963, one year—almost to the day—after Marilyn's death Jackie Kennedy gave birth to a boy. Born with respiratory problems, baby Patrick died two days later.

Unlike 1956 when Jack chose not to interrupt his Mediterranean holiday because Jackie suffered a miscarriage back home, in the summer of 1963 Jack was an exemplary husband and father. He took his ailing son to Children's Hospital in Boston and slept in the same room with Patrick, who died the next day. When Jack broke the news to his wife, he sobbed in her arms. "That was the only time I ever saw him cry," Jackie said. The day she left the hospital, reporters were shocked to see the President and the First Lady holding hands as they walked to their car.

Though Jack was seeing Mary Meyer and other women, he was also beginning to fully appreciate Jackie as a wife and valuable asset to his political image. White House observers said the tragedy of Patrick's death brought them closer together.

Jackie had made thirteen trips abroad as First Lady, but refused to travel with Jack on official business within the United States. He did not *tell* her she *had* to accompany him to Dallas.

Instead, Jack *asked* her, and she told a friend, "I'll hate every minute of it, but if Jack wants me there, I'm going."

Jackie was miffed about the President's refusal to use the bubble top on their car in Dallas. She complained about the heat and what her hair would look like when they arrived at the Trade Mart for a luncheon. Jack wanted the people of Dallas to see them and told his wife not to wear dark glasses because "the people want to see your face."

Jackie, who was looking in another direction, turned and saw the shocked expression on the President's face. He grasped his throat and slumped into her lap. Bits of brain matter, pieces of his skull and blood splattered on Jackie's pink suit. "My God, what are they doing?" she screamed. "My God, they've killed Jack, they've killed my husband … Jack, Jack!"

Jacqueline Kennedy's cousin, author John H. Davis, said, "At the time he died, I too was idealistic about JFK. Now, whenever I see those old films of Kennedy on television, I have to stop myself from heaving. It's hard to believe that here was this absolute fake, this womanizer and opportunist, coming off like Euripides. All our dreams invested in that! What a disappointment!"

After John Kennedy's assassination, Bobby's aim was to be a contender for the vice-presidential nomination on the Democratic ticket. But President Lyndon Johnson did not want a Kennedy in the White House, and disqualified members of his cabinet from running for the vice presidency in 1964.

Bobby resigned and announced his candidacy for U.S. Senator from New York. He won by a landslide in November.

John Davis believes that Robert Kennedy knew deep in his heart that his relentless efforts to "get Castro" and destroy the Mafia had resulted in the destruction of his own brother. This caused a suicidal sense of guilt to become lodged in his soul.

Bobby told a friend, "I don't know why God put us on earth. If I had my choice I would never have lived."

In the mid sixties, Bobby was consumed with his quest for the presidency. He spent time with Jackie, who was now living on Fifth Avenue in New York City. They were seen so much together, tongues began to wag. Jackie heard the rumors and fueled them by holding hands with Bobby or hugging and kissing him in public. He was good natured about it, smiling or responding with warmth. This was not like Bobby, but he needed Jackie's support to sit in the Oval Office.

In 1968, Kennedy was beginning his campaign for the presidential nomination when Jackie dropped a bomb. She was contemplating marriage to Aristotle Onassis. Bobby took the news very badly because he knew the American people held his brother's widow in such high esteem. They would be appalled if she married "the Greek." Bobby asked Jackie to postpone her plans for a few months until he won the nomination. She agreed.

On June 5, Kennedy won a major victory in California. After giving his thank-you speech at the Ambassador Hotel in Los Angeles, Bobby shouted to his supporters, "On to Chicago. Let's win there!" Ethel Kennedy, pregnant with their eleventh child, stood proudly at his side. Rushing to a press conference in the Colonial Room, Bobby ducked through the pantry followed by his wife and aides. Waiting for Kennedy was Sirhan Sirhan, who fired eight rounds from his pistol, hitting Bobby in the head and wounding five other people.

Twenty-six hours later, Robert F. Kennedy died at the Good Samaritan Hospital in Los Angeles.

Just prior to Bobby's assassination, an independent Republican group called journalist Ralph De Toledano about the Kennedy-Monroe tapes. He got in touch with a policeman who offered to sell them for $50,000. De Toledano told both parties to work out their own deal, but he wanted no part of it. The arrangements were made, but that same night Bobby was killed.

*

Peter Lawford's marriage ended not long after the president's assassination. Pat took their four children back East and got a divorce. Peter remarried three times. He was heavily dependent on cocaine, assorted drugs and alcohol that not only drained him financially, but killed him in 1984 at the age of sixty-one. His crypt in Westwood Mortuary was near Marilyn's, a fact that would have amused him, said widow Patricia Seaton Lawford. Four years later, however, she had to remove Peter's ashes from the crypt because his funeral expenses, amounting to $10,000, had not been paid.

Patricia contacted Lawford's children, who decided Peter just "wasn't worth it" and sent her a check for $430 to cover the disinterment fees. Patricia removed the urn from Peter's crypt in Westwood Mortuary and scattered his ashes at sea.

The Kennedys waited until the ghoulish deed was done and issued a statement that the bills had been paid. For peace of mind Patricia asked to see the receipts, but the mortuary denied her request.

Sam Giancana was murdered in 1975, shot seven times—first in the back of the head, then in the mouth and neck. His daughter, Antoinette ("The Mafia Princess"), was sure her father was killed by the same people responsible for killing the Kennedys—the CIA.

Eleven days after Giancana's murder, Teamster boss Jimmy Hoffa disappeared and was never found. A government informant associated with organized crime said after Hoffa was killed, his body was crushed by a compactor for wrecked cars to become sheet metal.

Shortly after Giancana's death, a corpse, whose legs had been sawed off, was found in an oil drum that was floating off Biscayne Bay in Florida. The body was identified as Giancana's lieutenant on the West Coast, Johnny Roselli, also a friend of

Marilyn's. He had been strangled to death.

All of these men were indirectly linked to Marilyn Monroe's death, a death that was peaceful in comparison to those who toyed with her life.

What goes around comes around. . . .

25

Body and Soul

There were many men in Marilyn's life, but they all adored the playful little girl with a woman's body. Though many will disagree, she was never vulgar. Nor was Marilyn a whore, oversexed or an opportunist. She warmed-up the casting couch, but Marilyn was honest about it—which is more than can be said for other movie queens.

On his deathbed, Joe Schenck asked to see Marilyn one last time. When they met, he was one of the most powerful moguls in Hollywood. Schenck could have had any woman he wanted to satisfy his sexual needs. Marilyn was there to service him, but he received much more from her playful spirit and gaiety than he did from a limp climax.

Marilyn's affair with agent Johnny Hyde best represents her outlook on life. "I don't care for money. I just want to be wonderful," she said. How many women would have turned down Hyde's marriage proposal? He had millions and wasn't expected to live much longer. Besides the money, she could have had his name, which demanded respect from everyone in show business.

But Marilyn had to marry for love. She searched for her father in the guise of Sir Lancelot, but when these heroes shed their shining armor, they turned out not to be her gallant and brave defenders. With two black eyes, Marilyn faced the world alone to announce her divorce from Joe DiMaggio.

Arthur Miller ignored and rejected Marilyn. In the end he realized his role of father might save her, but would surely destroy him. He walked out and Marilyn had a nervous breakdown.

Bob Slatzer's marriage to Marilyn might have lasted. They were victims of bad timing that can be chalked up to fate as his not being in Los Angeles on August 4, 1962. Slatzer ignored DiMaggio's spotlight and proved his devotion to Marilyn over the past thirty years by tirelessly investigating her mysterious death.

Marilyn's love for musician Fred Karger was an important factor in her life and, for a long time, she carried a torch for him. In his own way he, too, cared very much about her. Karger refused to play at a reception for the President in 1960 because he was sickened by the way the Kennedys were using Marilyn.

Marlon Brando talked to her frequently during the last week of her life. He refuses to discuss their conversations, but he was another former lover who remained a friend.

Yves Montand's film career blossomed following his highly publicized affair with Marilyn, and he enjoyed romances with some of his other famous leading ladies as well. While making *My Geisha* in Japan, he allegedly had an affair with co-star Shirley MacLaine. Soon after Simone Signoret's death from cancer in 1985, Yves began appearing in public with his young secretary Carole Amiel, and in 1988 she gave birth to their son Valentin. Montand said, "I am mad with joy," but his happiness was shortlived. He suffered a heart attack on November 8, 1991. Before Yves died the following day he said, "I have lived well enough to have no regrets."

Marilyn had faith only in her body, which is more psychological than sexual. Photographer Bert Stern, who took pictures of her for *Vogue*, shortly before she died, had some interesting comments: "Marilyn didn't have any good features, actually. She didn't have a good nose, or good eyes—or anything—but she was gorgeous, her spirit and all things together. . . . She was pure—so untouched, really like a virgin in many ways. But she wanted very deeply to show herself—her beauty and her body."

> *I'm a failure as a woman.*
> *Men expect so much and I can't live up to it.*
> —MARILYN MONROE (1962)

Epilogue

I chose not to elaborate on the details of Marilyn Monroe's death because my theme revolved around the men in her life. But I had to delve into the extensive research that was brilliantly done by authors Robert Slatzer, Anthony Summers, Fred Lawrence Guiles, Norman Mailer, and James Spada. The reader will find their books listed in the bibliography.

I agree with Ayn Rand, who said, "Anyone who has ever felt resentment against the good for being the good, and has given voice to it, is the murderer of Marilyn Monroe."

Jane Ellen Wayne
1992

Marilyn Monroe Filmography

Dangerous Years
(20th Century-Fox, 1947)

Producer: Sol M. Wurtzel
Director: Arthur Pierson
Editor: Frank Balridge
Cast: Ann E. Todd, William Halop, Donald Curtis, Jerome
     Cowan, Darryl Hickman, Scotty Beckett, Dickie Moore,
     Richard Gaines, Marilyn Monroe
Black and White, 62 minutes

Scudda Hoo! Scudda Hay!
(20th Century-Fox, 1948)

Producer: Walter Morosco
Director: F. Hugh Herbert
Editor: Harmon Jones
Cast: June Haver, Lon McCallister, Anne Revere, Walter
     Brennan, Natalie Wood (Marilyn did not receive screen
     credit)
Technicolor, 95 minutes

Ladies of the Chorus
(Columbia Pictures, 1948)

Producer: Harry A. Romm
Director: Phil Karlson
Editor: Richard Fantl

Cast: Adele Jergens, Rand Brooks, Marilyn Monroe, Eddie
 Garr, Nana Bryant, Steven Geray
Black and White, 61 minutes

Love Happy
(Presented by Mary Pickford, 1949)
Released by United Artists

Producer: Lester Cowan
Director: David Miller
Editors: Basil Wrangell and Al Joseph
Story: Harpo Marx
Cast: Groucho Marx, Chico Marx, Harpo Marx, Ilona Massey,
 Vera-Ellen, Raymond Burr, Marion Hutton, Marilyn
 Monroe
Black and White, 85 minutes

A Ticket to Tomahawk
(20th Century-Fox, 1950)

Producer: Robert Bassler
Director: Richard Sale
Editor: Harmon Jones
Cast: Dan Dailey, Anne Baxter, Walter Brennan, Rory
 Calhoun, Will Wright, Connie Gilchrist, Marilyn
 Monroe
Technicolor, 90 minutes

The Asphalt Jungle
(MGM, 1950)

Producer: Arthur Hornblow, Jr.
Director: John Huston
Editor: George Boemler
Cast: Sterling Hayden, Sam Jaffee, Louis Calhern, Jean
 Hagen, James Whitmore, Marilyn Monroe
Black and White, 112 minutes

All About Eve
(20th Century-Fox, 1950)

Producer: Darryl F. Zanuck
Director: Joseph L. Mankiewicz
Editor: Barbara McLean
Cast: Bette Davis, Anne Baxter, Celeste Holm, George Sanders, Gary Merrill, Marilyn Monroe
Black and White, 130 minutes

The Fireball
(Thor Production, 1950)
Released by 20th Century-Fox

Producer: Bert Friedlob
Director: Tay Garnett
Editor: Frank Sullivan
Cast: Mickey Rooney, Glenn Corbett, Beverly Tyler, Pat O'Brien, Marilyn Monroe
Black and White, 84 minutes

Right Cross
(MGM, 1950)

Producer: Armand Deutsch
Director: John Sturges
Editor: James Newcom
Cast: Dick Powell, June Allyson, Ricardo Montalban, Lionel Barrymore, Larry Keating (Marilyn Monroe did not receive screen credit)
Black and White, 90 minutes

Hometown Story
(MGM, 1951)

Producer: Arthur Pierson
Director: Arthur Pierson
Editor: William Claxton
Cast: Donald Crisp, Jeffrey Lynn, Marjorie Reynolds, Alan
      Hale, Jr., Marilyn Monroe
Black and White, 61 minutes

As Young As You Feel
(20th Century-Fox, 1951)

Producer: Lamar Trotti
Director: Harmon Jones
Editor: Robert Simpson
Cast: Thelma Ritter, David Wayne, Monty Woolley, Jean
      Peters, Constance Bennett, Marilyn Monroe
Black and White, 77 minutes

Love Nest
(20th Century-Fox, 1951)

Producer, Jules Buck
Director: Joseph Newman
Editor: J. Watson Webb, Jr.
Cast: William Lundigan, June Haver, Marilyn Monroe, Frank
      Fay, Jack Paar, Leatrice Joy
Black and White, 84 minutes

Let's Make It Legal
(20th Century-Fox, 1951)

Producer: Robert Bassler
Director: Richard Sale
Editor: Robert Fritch
Cast: Claudette Colbert, Zachary Scott, Barbara Bates,
     Macdonald Carey, Robert Wagner, Marilyn Monroe
Black and White, 77 minutes

Clash by Night
(Jerry Wald–Norman Krasna Production, 1952)
Released by RKO

Producer: Harriet Parsons
Director: Fritz Lang
Editor: George J. Amy
Story: Clifford Odets
Cast: Paul Douglas, Barbara Stanwyck, Robert Ryan, Marilyn
     Monroe
Black and White, 105 minutes

We're Not Married
(20th Century-Fox, 1952)

Producer: Nunnally Johnson
Director: Edmund Goulding
Editor: Louis Loeffler
Cast: Ginger Rogers, Marilyn Monroe, Victor Mature, Fred
     Allen, David Wayne, Eve Arden, Mitzi Gaynor
Black and White, 85 minutes

Don't Bother to Knock
(20th Century-Fox, 1952)

Producer: Julian Blaustein
Director: Roy Baker
Editor: George A. Gittens
Cast: Marilyn Monroe, Richard Widmark, Anne Bancroft, Jeanne Cagney, Jim Backus
Black and White, 76 minutes

Monkey Business
(20th Century-Fox, 1952)

Producer: Sol C. Siegel
Director: Howard Hawks
Editor: William B. Murphy
Cast: Cary Grant, Ginger Rogers, Charles Colburn, Marilyn Monroe, Hugh Marlowe
Black and White, 97 minutes

O. Henry's Full House
(20th Century-Fox, 1952)

Producer: Andre Hakim
Director: Kenry Koster
Story: O. Henry (from "The Cop and the Anthem")
Cast: Charles Laughton, Marilyn Monroe, David Wayne
Black and White, 71 minutes

Niagara
(20th Century-Fox, 1953)

Producer: Charles Brackett
Director: Henry Hathaway
Editor: Barbara McLean

Cast: Joseph Cotten, Marilyn Monroe, Jean Peters, Casey
    Adams, Russell Collins
Technicolor, 89 minutes

Gentlemen Prefer Blondes
(20th Century-Fox, 1953)

Producer: Sol C. Siegel
Director: Howard Hawks
Editor: Hugh S. Wynn
Musical Score: Lionel Newman
Story: Anita Loos and Joseph Fields
Cast: Jane Russell, Marilyn Monroe, Charles Coburn, Elliott
    Reid, Tommy Noonan
Technicolor, 91 minutes

How to Marry a Millionaire
(20th Century-Fox, 1953)

Producer: Nunnally Johnson
Director: Jean Negulesco
Editor: Louis Loeffler
Cast: Betty Grable, Lauren Bacall, Marilyn Monroe, David
    Wayne, William Powell, Fred Clark, Rory Calhoun,
    Cameron Mitchell
CinemaScope and Technicolor, 96 minutes

River of No Return
(20th Century-Fox, 1954)

Producer: Stanley Rubin
Director: Otto Preminger
Editor: Louis Loeffler
Cast: Robert Mitchum, Marilyn Monroe, Rory Calhoun,
    Tommy Rettig
CinemaScope and Technicolor, 91 minutes

There's No Business Like Show Business
(20th Century-Fox, 1954)

Producer: Sol C. Siegel
Director: Walter Lang
Editor: Robert Simpson
Cast: Ethel Merman, Dan Dailey, Donald O'Connor, Marilyn
     Monroe, Mitzi Gaynor, Johnnie Ray, Hugh O'Brian
CinemaScope and Color by Deluxe, 117 minutes

The Seven Year Itch
(20th Century-Fox, 1955)

Producers: Charles K. Feldman and Billy Wilder
Director: Billy Wilder
Editor: Hugh S. Fowler
Cast: Tom Ewell, Marilyn Monroe, Evelyn Keyes, Sonny
     Tufts
CinemaScope and Color by Deluxe, 105 minutes

Bus Stop
(20th Century-Fox, 1956)

Producer: Buddy Adler
Director: Joshua Logan
Editor: William Reynolds
Cast: Marilyn Monroe, Don Murray, Betty Field, Hope
     Lange, Arthur O'Connell, Eileen Heckart
CinemaScope and Color by Deluxe, 96 minutes

The Prince and the Showgirl
(Marilyn Monroe Productions, 1957)
Released through Warner Brothers

Producer: Laurence Olivier
Director: Laurence Olivier
Editor: Jack Harris
Cast: Laurence Olivier, Marilyn Monroe, Jeremy Spenser, Dame Sybil Thorndike
Technicolor, 117 minutes

Some Like It Hot
(Mirisch Company–Ashton Pictures, 1959)
Released through United Artists

Producer: Billy Wilder
Director: Billy Wilder
Editor: Arthur Schmidt
Cast: Marilyn Monroe, Tony Curtis, Jack Lemmon, Pat O'Brien, George Raft, Joe E. Brown
Black and White, 120 minutes

Let's Make Love
(20th Century-Fox, 1960)

Producer: Jerry Wald
Director: George Cukor
Editor: David Bretherton
Cast: Marilyn Monroe, Yves Montand, Frankie Vaughan, Tony Randall. **Guest Stars:** Milton Berle, Gene Kelly, Bing Crosby
CinemaScope and Color by Deluxe, 118 minutes

The Misfits
(Seven Arts–John Huston Production, 1961)
Released through United Artists

Producer: Frank E. Taylor
Director: John Huston
Editor: George Tomasini
Screenplay: Arthur Miller
Cast: Clark Gable, Marilyn Monroe, Montgomery Clift, Thelma Ritter, Eli Wallach
Black and White, 124 minutes

Something's Got to Give
(20th Century-Fox)
Unfinished. Shelved in June of 1962

Producer: Henry Weinstein
Director: George Cukor
Cast: Marilyn Monroe, Dean Martin, Cyd Charisse, Wally Cox, Phil Silvers.

Selected Bibliography

Austin, John. *Hollywood's Unsolved Mysteries*. New York: Shapolsky Books, 1990.

Bacall, Lauren. *By Myself*. New York: Alfred A. Knopf, 1979.

Bacon, James. *Hollywood Is a Four Letter Town*. Chicago: Henry Regnery Co., 1976.

Brynner, Rock. *Yul: The Man Who Would Be King*. New York: Simon and Schuster, 1989.

Carpozi, George. *Marilyn Monroe, Her Own Story*. New York: Belmont Books, 1961.

Carpozi, George. *The Agony of Marilyn Monroe*. London: World Distributors, 1962.

Cassini, Oleg. *In My Fashion*. New York: Simon and Schuster, 1987.

Conover, David. *Finding Marilyn: A Romance*. New York: Gosset & Dunlap, 1981.

Conway, Michael and Mark Ricci. *The Films of Marilyn Monroe*. Secaucus, NJ: Citadel Press, 1964.

Davis, John H. *The Kennedys*. New York: McGraw-Hill Book Company, 1984.

Desser, Lloyd Fuller. *The Illustrated Who's Who of the Cinema*. London: Orbin Publishing Ltd., 1983.

Dougherty, James E. *The Secret Happiness of Marilyn Monroe*. Chicago: Playboy Press, 1976.

Eells, George. *Hedda and Louella*. New York: G. P. Putnam's Sons, 1972.

————. *Robert Mitchum*. New York: Franklin Watts, 1984.

Finler, Joel W. *The Movie Director's Story*. London: Octopus Books Ltd., 1985.

Franklin, Joe, and Laurie Palmer. *The Marilyn Monroe Story.* Chicago: Field Enterprises, 1953.

Goode, James. *Making of* The Misfits. New York: Bob Merrill Co., 1963.

Goodman, Ezra. *The Fifty-Year Decline and Fall of Hollywood.* New York: Simon and Schuster, 1961.

Graham, Sheila. *Hollywood Revisited.* New York: St. Martin's Press, 1984.

Guiles, Fred Lawrence. *Norma Jean.* New York: McGraw-Hill, 1969.

———. *Legend: The Life and Death of Marilyn Monroe.* New York: Stein and Day, 1984.

Halliwell, Leslie. *The Filmgoer's Companion.* New York: Hill and Wang, 1977.

———. *Halliwell's Film Guide.* New York: Harper & Row, 1989.

Heymann, David C. *A Woman Named Jackie.* New York: Lyle Stuart, Inc., 1989.

Higham, Charles and Roy Mosley. *Cary Grant: The Lonely Heart.* New York: Harcourt Brace Jovanovich, 1989.

Huston, John. *An Open Book.* New York: Alfred A. Knopf Inc., 1980.

Hyams, Joe. *Misled in Hollywood.* New York: Peter H. Wyden, Inc., 1973.

Kahn, Roger. *Joe and Marilyn: A Memory of Love.* New York: William Morrow & Co., 1986.

Kelley, Kitty. *Jackie Oh!* Secaucus, NJ: Lyle Stuart, Inc., 1978.

———. *Elizabeth Taylor: The Last Star.* New York: Simon & Schuster, 1981.

———. *His Way: The Unauthorized Biography of Frank Sinatra.* New York: Bantam, 1986.

Kobal, John. *People Will Talk.* New York: Alfred A. Knopf Inc., 1986.

LaGuardia, Robert. *Monty: A Biography of Montgomery Clift.* New York: Arbor House, 1977.

Lawford, Patricia Seaton. *The Peter Lawford Story*. New York: Carroll & Graf Publishers, Inc., 1988.

Michael, Paul. *The American Movies*. New York: Prentice-Hall, 1970.

Mailer, Norman. *Marilyn: A Biography*. New York: Grosset and Dunlap, 1972.

Monroe, Marilyn. *My Story*. New York: Stein and Day, 1974.

Murray, Eunice. *Marilyn: The Last Months*. New York: Pyramid, 1975.

Olivier, Laurence. *Confessions of an Actor*. New York: Simon & Schuster, 1982.

Pastos, Spero. *Pin-Up: The Tragedy of Betty Grable*. New York: G. P. Putman's Sons, 1986.

Pepitone, Lena. *Marilyn Monroe Confidential*. New York: Simon & Schuster, 1979.

Rooney, Mickey. *Life Is Too Short*. New York: Villard Books, 1991.

Rosten, Norman. *Marilyn: The Untold Story*. New York: Signet, 1973.

Russell, Jane. *Jane Russell: An Autobiography*. New York: Franklin Watts, Inc., 1985.

Sciacca, Tony. *Who Killed Marilyn?* New York: Manor Books, 1976.

Shevey, Sandra. *The Marilyn Scandal*. London: Sidgwick & Jackson, 1986.

Slatzer, Robert. *The Life and Curious Death of Marilyn Monroe*. Los Angeles: Pinnacle, 1974.

Smith, Ella. *Starring Miss Barbara Stanwyck*. New York: Crown Publishers, 1974.

Spada, James. *Peter Lawford: The Man Who Kept the Secrets*. New York: Bantam, 1991.

Speriglio, Milo. *Marilyn Monroe Murder Cover-up*. Van Nuys, CA: Seville Publishing, 1982.

————. *The Marilyn Conspiracy*. New York: Pocket Books, Simon & Schuster 1986.

Steinem, Gloria. *Marilyn—Norma Jean*. New York: Henry Holt & Co., 1986.

Sullivan, Michael John. *Presidential Passions*. New York: Shapolsky, 1991.

Summers, Anthony. *Goddess: The Secret Lives of Marilyn Monroe*. New York: Macmillan Publishing, 1985.

Swanson, Gloria. *Swanson on Swanson*. New York: Random House, 1980.

Thomas, Bob. *Joan Crawford*. New York: Simon & Schuster, 1978.

Tierney, Gene. *Self-Portrait*. New York: Wyden Books, 1976.

Tormé, Mel. *It Wasn't All Velvet*. New York: Viking, 1988.

Tornabene, Lyn. *Long Live the King: A Biography of Clark Gable*. New York: G. P. Putman's Sons, 1976.

Wagenlnecht, Edward. *Marilyn Monroe: A Composite View*. Philadelphia: Chilton Book Co., 1969.

Wayne, Jane Ellen. *Gable's Women*. New York: Prentice-Hall, 1987.

Wiener, Leigh. *Marilyn Monroe: A Hollywood Farewell*. Los Angeles: 7410 Publishing Co., 1990.

Winters, Shelley. *Shelley II*. New York: Simon & Schuster, 1989.

Zolotow, Maurice. *Marilyn Monroe*. New York: Harcourt, Brace and Co., 1960.

Index

Famous Lives

from St. Martin's Paperbacks

LIBERACE: THE TRUE STORY
Bob Thomas
_____ 91352-4 $3.95 U.S. _____ 91354-0 $4.95 Can.

THE FITZGERALDS AND THE KENNEDYS
Doris Kearns Goodwin
_____ 90933-0 $5.95 U.S. _____ 90934-9 $6.95 Can.

CAROLINE AND STEPHANIE
Susan Crimp and Patricia Burstein
_____ 91116-5 $3.50 U.S. _____ 91117-3 $4.50 Can.

PATRICK SWAYZE
Mitchell Krugel
_____ 91449-0 $3.50 U.S. _____ 91450-4 $4.50 Can.

YOUR CHEATIN' HEART:
A BIOGRAPHY OF HANK WILLIAMS
Chet Flippo
_____ 91400-8 $3.95 U.S. _____ 91401-6 $4.95 Can.

WHO'S SORRY NOW?
Connie Francis
_____ 90386-3 $3.95 U.S. _____ 90383-9 $4.95 Can.

MEET THE SUPERSTARS
With St. Martin's Paperbacks!

PRISCILLA,
ELVIS
AND ME

The sizzling, sensational love story that starts where Priscilla Presley's bestselling autobiography left off!

PRISCILLA, ELVIS AND ME

MICHAEL EDWARDS

Michael Edwards' passionate romance with Priscilla Presley burned hot and fast. From the early, heady days of sexual passion and romantic bliss, to the terrible fights sparked by Lisa Marie's blossoming womanhood, *Priscilla, Elvis and Me* is a love story that is wrenching in its honesty and unflinching in its telling—an intimate look at a "perfect" love in a frozen moment of time...in the shadow of a legend.

With 16 pages of intimate photos!

BESTSELLING BOOKS FROM ST. MARTIN'S PAPERBACKS— TO READ AND READ AGAIN!

NOT WITHOUT MY DAUGHTER
Betty Mahmoody with William Hoffer
_____ 92588-3 $5.95 U.S./$6.95 Can.

PROBABLE CAUSE
Ridley Pearson
_____ 92385-6 $5.95 U.S./$6.95 Can.

RIVERSIDE DRIVE
Laura Van Wormer
_____ 91572-1 $5.95 U.S.   _____ 91574-8 $6.95 Can.

SHADOW DANCERS
Herbert Lieberman
_____ 92288-4 $5.95 U.S./$6.95 Can.

THE FITZGERALDS AND THE KENNEDYS
Doris Kearns Goodwin
_____ 90933-0 $5.95 U.S.   _____ 90934-9 $6.95 Can.

JAMES HERRIOT'S DOG STORIES
James Herriot
_____ 92558-1 $5.99 U.S.